BE THE DANCE TEACHER
THEY REMEMBER

From Dancing to Teaching, Classical
Ballet Pedagogy in Practice

By Candace Egbert

Dedicated to Chandler. Your support means the world to me.

*Note: All of the terminology spelling in this book comes from the book *Technical Manual and Dictionary of Classical Ballet, Third revised edition,* by Gail Grant
**Photographs by Candace Egbert; models Ella Brucker and Abby Lindley

Cover artwork/design: Sarah Spicer

Copy Editor: Natalie Johnson

Contact: candace.m.egbert@gmail.com

ISBN 979-8-9865337-0-4 (paperback), ISBN 979-8-9865337-1-1(ebook)

"Teaching is a very noble profession that shapes the character, caliber, and future of an individual. If the people remember me as a good teacher that will be the biggest honour for me."

-A. P. J. Abdul Kalam

Foreword

"I danced professionally for fifteen years and have taught dance for almost thirty years. It was a pleasure reading this excellent addition to the ballet/dance pedagogy catalog. The author has written a broad reaching reflection on the value and artistry of dance instruction. She offers practical as well as philosophical guidance that can easily be transferred into the studio. This book would be a fine companion to any of the numerous instruction manuals that highlight dance curricular exercises. Novice teachers should gain confidence in stepping into the studio, and experienced instructors will no doubt receive a boost of enthusiasm for their work."

-Mark Borchelt

"I owned a dance studio in California just north of Santa Barbara and taught dance for 17 years. I loved reading Candace's book and I highly recommend it! I was so impressed with all her practical, teaching advice. It was easy to read and organized perfectly. The book really breaks down the art of teaching in such a spectacular way to make teaching more joyful for both the teacher and the student. I believe it has changed the way I would now teach dance! Thank you Candace!"

-Bonnie Olson

Contents

Introduction

Picture in your mind the teachers who changed everything for you. For me, it was the few teachers who made me feel challenged and accomplished at the same time. I wanted to do my best so they would be proud of me. They left a legacy of inspired students, including me.

Since I became a dance teacher, I have heard those teachers' voices echo in my mind and in the things I emphasize to my own students. They shaped me in more ways than I can express

As teachers, we closely mirror the lessons we learned as students. The lessons become built into our subconscious, and it is easiest to emulate what we experienced. But if we want our dance students to be more driven and accomplished, there needs to be more intentional dance teaching coming from us. We cannot keep repeating the rituals passed down through generations of dance teachers–at least not for the sake of tradition alone.

It's likely you are not new to the dance world. You have probably found some things that work for you as a dancer, and you have discovered what doesn't work through your own trial and error. But being a dancer alone does not qualify someone to be a dance teacher. Exceptional dancers don't always transition seamlessly into extraordinary teachers.

A standard teacher training path is somewhat of a luxury if you come from a more public/local dance education. And dancers too often jump into the role of "teacher" with relatively little experience in training dancers or directing a class.

So I aim to supplement that gap for those who don't have the opportunity to formally learn to become exceptional teachers.

This book has roots extending back several years to my college days majoring in ballet performance. I didn't think much about it at the time, but I wish we spent more time formally learning how to teach. I think there were only a handful of pedagogy-specific courses in my entire four-year program.

I had many knowledgeable and caring professors who taught me a great deal.

And though I thought the program was well-rounded, I wished for more experience knowing how to translate it into my classes when I became an instructor. And considering that the majority of us became teachers (whether we were dancing professionally or not), we would have benefited from a more in-depth education on teaching.

But this book is not a critique of my university program. Instead, my experience is a snapshot of the broader issue of dancers who become teachers without adequate training in pedagogy. Because outside the realm of classical ballet school curriculums or getting an education-specific degree, there aren't many formal schooling options to become a dance teacher–at least that is the case in much of the United States.

Teaching is a learned skill

I want my students to leave the studio with better technique, work ethic, attention to detail, and perseverance. I am sure you want that for your students as well. And though it is easy to become overwhelmed with the dance world's many methodologies and training philosophies, there are universal truths that can guide all teaching.

Thinking about the teachers who left an impact on us, it may seem that they were born with an innate ability to direct a class and relate to their students–drawing the best work from them. But those skills aren't just innate abilities. Great teaching is a skill that can be learned.

This book will give you a glimpse into how to create the best studio environment for your students. A ripe studio environment looks like:

- laying a foundation of the basics,

- adapting teaching when necessary,

- engaging students to invest in their own learning,

- and loving your students.

You will be able to build an environment where your dancers can learn the lasting truths that will carry them as far as they wish in the dance world–even positively impacting other parts of their lives.

The best dancers are molded to be artists, not imitators of their predecessors. And the aspects that make a good teacher are relevant even as old practices such as discrimination based on body type, race, or gender fall away.

Who this book is for

This book may find a comfortable home as an aid for newer teachers, but it can benefit teachers from varying levels of experience.

I wrote this book initially for people like me. I have been removed from the realm of formal education and performing for several years now. Yet, I still want to make a difference in the lives of my students, even though teaching is not my only pursuit. I am a wife, mother, family chef, kid chauffeur, active churchgoer and volunteer, and housekeeper, *and* I want to be a caring and effective dance teacher. I recognize many of my peers are also former dancers with their own growing families and responsibilities outside of dance and they are navigating balancing those roles as well.

But this book will benefit dance teachers at various stages. It is a resource for:

- the former-dancer-turned-teacher,

- the burned-out teacher needing a refocus,

- teachers who may no longer be completing curriculum training or degree programs to refine their skills,

- and teachers who never even chose to pursue a dance degree or found their program lacking in this area.

So, if you have felt a similar need to translate your dance knowledge into usable teaching tools, this book is for you. Whether you instruct twenty classes a semester, or just one, this book is for you.

What to expect from these pages

You will find that this book is not full of ground-breaking research for dance teachers. It does not bring to light any revolutionary studies or a brand new curriculum. Nor does it dissect all aspects of pedagogy or technique for any one particular genre of dance.

Instead, this book is a thoughtful gathering of relatable personal experiences that will help with overall conceptual teaching and class management. It's an honest confession of trial and error and trial and success.

This book is not an all-in-one bible for teachers. My experience does not extend to the upper echelons of the world's dance training academies. And even though the bulk of my experience is primarily as a ballet teacher in local schools and privately owned studios, the concepts apply across many studio settings and genres of dance. I tried to strike a balance and cover overarching concepts without making the mistake of oversimplifying the many facets of dance training.

My Hope for You

I hope that the ideas in these pages solidify your resolve to become a better teacher than you are now—to be more deliberate. My hope is to help well-intentioned dance teachers to become more than well-intentioned.

Not everything written here will work for everyone, but there is something here for you. I hope that this little book can be a valuable resource and a reminder of *how* to teach, not just a glossary of *what* to teach.

I hope you see yourself in the experiences I share and they can work as a mirror for deeper reflection and improvement in your teaching. Let us resolve to leave each of our dancers better than we found them.

1

Teach the Basics Unapologetically

Formative lessons cannot be redone

A COUPLE OF YEARS ago, I attended a teacher meeting before the start of the dance year. The meeting was for the ballet instructors teaching beginning levels that year. I was scheduled to teach two classes of young beginners and one class of a bit older beginning students. I was excited for the fresh start and change of pace after teaching intermediate and advanced dancers for several years previously.

Our ballet director usually used those yearly meetings to go over the curriculum of steps the dancers are expected to learn at their level and allow us to share any teaching tips with each other.

After our usual chatting and catching up, our director presented the updated and refined curriculum for the year. Rather than just a list of steps for the dancers to master, she wanted to go over specific exercises that we would use to teach certain steps. It struck me when she asked us to use only those specific exercises all year.

My first thought was: *How in the world will I use these exact exercises every week for the entire year?* Second, I was worried about my ability to keep the dancers interested. They were young students, after all. *Wouldn't they get bored?*

I admit that was a knee-jerk reaction. But I already knew it, focusing on those crucial foundations was spot-on.

Formative lessons cannot be rewound and redone. I knew a dancer's first experiences in class would set the stage for their attention to detail later.

I wasn't new to teaching, but that guidance was the reminder and push I needed. It was a small but impactful lesson. Careful repetition is the key to learning something deeply.

I decided to take on the challenge. So, instead of rushing through those foundations of movement, I embraced the chance to teach the same exercises over and over. The only adaptations I allowed myself were various verbal and physical cues we explored as a class. The exercises themselves did not change.

It was freeing to have permission to slow down. It's hard not to feel rushed in the dance world when you know how much there is ahead of you to learn. I was used to thinking that there is never enough time in the studio. But instead, I had the opportunity to focus on what was necessary without rushing–which is a rare feeling.

We kept the exercises the same all year. Pliés always began with a preparation and hands to the barre. They were slowly descending and slowly ascending every time. The counts were the same in every class. Tendus were the same as well. First, we started devant, and once the students mastered that, we added á la seconde and then finally derrière. All the while, the exercise was the same. We kept consistency for all of our combinations.

I used that repetition to create a space where the dancers could understand the movement entirely. They knew why we did pliés a certain way because we explored many ways to think about a simple plié. They knew what a tendu looked like and felt like, and they did their tendus with more purpose than other more advanced dancers I have taught. They were discovering each step and exploring them fully with different images and focuses in mind.

Those dancers started with a strong foundation, thanks to the wisdom of our astute ballet director. I am grateful I didn't miss the opportunity to give that foundation to them.

Now, does every class need to run this way? No. Dancers need to learn to adapt, of course. At some point, we have to push them to become better. But our students can't build themselves without the underlying basics first.

One of the main focuses and inspirations for this book is this very thing. Simplify your teaching. Lay the groundwork, and it will pay off. Your dancers will be more successful inside and outside the studio if you do. They will leave the studio better off in more ways than you think.

Foundational Training

The foundations. The essentials. The groundwork. Everything a dancer does requires a working understanding of the basics. This understanding is true for any skill. Mastering the alphabet comes before reading. Learning the keys on the piano comes before playing any music. Laying a concrete foundation comes before building a house.

Likewise, solidifying the basics for your students is paramount. Even a successful person never leaves the basics after they learn them. Those fundamentals are built into everything they do. Even Mikhail Baryshnikov had to learn for himself how to utilize his plié correctly to defy gravity. Students need it, and we are doing them a disservice to gloss over the basics.

Focusing on the basics is not a new idea, but even seasoned teachers need this reminder and permission to re-focus. It's easy to fall into the trap of thoughtlessly going through the motions: warm-up, pliés, tendus, rélevés, etc. I sometimes find myself wanting to apologize to my students that we have to do pliés *again*. Or we have to get through this slow tendu exercise *again* before we can get to the more "fun" parts of technique class–modeling the attitude that those steps are somehow in the way of progress. As a result, I have rushed through these things and sometimes don't give them enough focus.

However, in more recent years, my inner mantra has become: *Teach the basics, and don't apologize for them.*

It is not uncommon to talk with other teachers (of varying disciplines) and lament how students these days are just not the same as they used to be. We are in such a fast-paced world, and our attention spans suffer because of it. With constant advances in technology and the prevalence of social media platforms, we are used to quick solutions and immediate feedback. And our students are in the thick of that conditioning. As a result, there is a real fear that our students will get bored and lose interest if we do not move quickly enough.

Do not give in to that fear.

One year I learned this lesson pretty clearly–it was pivotal in my growth as a teacher. I taught at a local studio and had a particularly challenging group of dancers. They didn't hide their lack of interest and often rolled their eyes with annoyance when they didn't like something I was demonstrating. They would talk on the side while I was giving instructions. Their attitude to some classmates was also disrespectful.

I was not a new teacher, and I know students have bad days. I know I am not a fun or engaging teacher all of the time either, but these were chronic issues with that particular class. The studio where I was teaching had a culture that discouraged that behavior, but I still struggled with those dancers.

It took a lot of mental energy to get ready to teach that group. I was used to being liked overall by my students, and I generally don't worry about what people think of me. And even though I knew my relationship with them was first to be a teacher, not a friend, I made a cardinal mistake. In a last-ditch effort to regain respect and supposedly save them from hating ballet, I tried to make nearly every moment of class "fun" and "exciting."

I found myself regularly apologizing for our time spent on the boring basics, and I tried to rush through them to get to the new and fun stuff. I let myself be intimidated. I lost sight of the bigger picture.

It was a problem, of course. In my efforts to make things only "fun," I didn't focus on building a solid foundation. As a result, when it came time to perform or get ready for auditions, many of those dancers were underperforming compared to previous students at that level.

They hadn't gained skills that were sticking. What's worse, I also had not required a certain level of respect or etiquette from them.

In my pursuit of chasing what I thought would interest them, I didn't give them what they needed. I feared my students' boredom and disapproval, and in avoiding that, I gave those students too much too fast.

Ironically, by the end of the dance year, I did not feel any more respect from those dancers than when I started. Instead of seeming relaxed or fun, I think I became wishy-washy and somewhat of a pushover in their eyes. I was not a good model for them.

It was hard not to feel like the year was just a wash. It did not feel like a fulfilling year for me, and most of those dancers weren't left any better than I found them. Many of them even left dance to pursue other interests the following year. Of course, much of the blame lies with those students for not putting forth the needed personal effort to improve, but I also needed to do my part as their teacher. It was my job to understand and envision the bigger picture and teach accordingly.

It is not a sin to want to give our students a fun experience. We don't want our students to hate coming to dance class–that misses the point. However, observing that clear cause and effect gave me more clarity in my role as a teacher. And I realized that skipping through the basics gave them a false idea of the effort and process it takes to improve as a dancer.

That experience taught me two specific things. One: I was naive to think that I needed to be liked by everyone for everything I do. I know that is not possible, and as a teacher, that can't be my number one goal. And two: I will never apologize for spending time on the basics again. They are too important. They lay the foundations for etiquette, safety, and ultimately success in the dance world.

This story is an anecdote from my personal life. Maybe you wouldn't make the same mistake I made. But the wisdom it gave me is worth repeating for anyone struggling to maintain that teacher/friend balance with their students. There is a battle between what we think our students want and what we know they need. My advice is to stick with what is essential–the rest will follow in time.

Students are more likely to grow in their respect for you as a teacher if you have a focused goal for them. Act as if your students care to be in class–even if it appears they don't. A student cannot be forced to care about working hard or persevering when things get complicated. It doesn't do them any favors to water things down or make excuses for what you are doing as the teacher.

You can teach desire to some degree, but it is more of an indirect lesson. Over time your students can learn to love dance *through* you. They will learn it from your consistent expectations and as they see the fruits of their efforts. Your enthusiasm for every aspect of dance–whether mundane or exciting–will provide an example for them to follow. They may not always realize it while they are in your class. But if in the future they look back on their time as your student, they will appreciate your resolve to give them a strong foundation.

The dissatisfaction with moving too quickly

Teach the basics and don't apologize for them because it is hard to go backward. Because once you decide to throw in 32 fouetté turns, switch leaps, triple pirouettes, and entrelacés before your students are ready or mature enough to value and execute the basics, they may become dissatisfied with the basics.

This principle is true in many aspects of life. If I give my kids the chance to play with friends or play computer games a few times before doing their homework and family jobs, they want that to be the new rule. They want to expect it and wonder why it can't always be that way–to play first and work later. Young children aren't mature or experienced enough to see why that is a problem. Adults also experience this struggle and often procrastinate until a deadline forces the work to happen.

A person's ability to delay gratification is an excellent skill to learn, but that doesn't make it easier to swallow. And it's a valuable lesson that we can teach in the studio.

You may decide that you love cookies for dessert so much that you will have a cookie or two after everything–breakfast, lunch, dinner, snacks, and so on. I love cookies, so this is easy for me to imagine.

For a time, that would be deliciously fun! But as time goes on, you would undoubtedly reap the consequences. You would start to grow weary of dessert. Your health would be affected. And dessert would have sadly lost its savor. It would no longer be a special treat–it would lose a lot of its intrigue.

Likewise, in dance class, having stretching parties, watching videos, playing games, using popular music, and only doing the dancers' favorite steps at their preferred speeds every other class will grow old and hinder development. It will not drive success. Those things can have their place in a dance class as a reward or an exception, but not as the regular expectation. They are the dessert in an otherwise balanced approach to training.

My son's school teaches a curriculum focused on the habits from the well-known book *7 Habits of Highly Effective People* written by Stephen Covey[1]. I have learned a lot from my son's simple perspective of those habits. He knows the habit of "putting first things first." He is learning the value of delaying gratification in favor of doing the work first for a greater reward. It's a lesson that benefits anyone who wants to persevere in developing any skill or attribute.

The lasting lessons from dance class come from pushing through the primary, repetitive, and seemingly monotonous steps. The undeniable hard work in the studio creates character, increases mental capacity, and molds the physical body beyond its natural form. Working in the studio brings genuine satisfaction. Those monotonous steps are the foundation that brings about great results.

In a way, directing your class is like flying a kite. A kite is a paradox. The kite only stays in flight because it is tethered to the ground. Cut that tether, and your kite will quickly plummet to the earth.

Likewise, you can fly far beyond the basics with your students, but your dancers still need to have that knowledge and muscle memory to tether them. They can move past the basics as soon as their tether to the basics is strong enough.

One more thing worth noting

It is also vital that anyone who teaches for you in a substituting capacity respects your desire to prioritize solid foundations.

In some studio settings, it is easy for a substitute teacher to come in and just do the fun steps and tricks with your students. But you know that consistent expectations are essential, so do your best to express to your substitute what matters to you. Then give them a clear and organized outline of what you expect.

There have been times when I have returned to class after an absence, and the dancers complained that we were "moving backward." They wonder why they got to do double and triple pirouettes with the substitute, but now they have to go back to cleaning up their position in their single pirouettes. And though this situation is not likely to happen in elite technical training schools, it can be more common in public or local smaller studio settings. Regardless, it is best to stick to what you know your students need.

To keep our students moving forward, we can't skip the necessary steps. I have seen students who advance too quickly through class levels. Maybe those students perform well at an audition, and then they are recommended to move up and skip a level. It is flattering to them, but it often leaves those students with gaps in their training that eventually become apparent. So much of that is difficult to rewind and redo.

Students will not ask for a slower pace, but as their guides, we can't in good conscience skip important learning by advancing our expectations of them faster than they are ready. And when that does happen, we need to be honest with them and keep an open dialogue about what those students still need to work on.

<u>Summary of Chapter One</u>

- Above all: *Teach the basics and don't apologize for them.*

- It is our job to lay a strong foundation of the basics for our students to build upon.

- There are a few reasons we may stray from the basics: fear of wasting time or not moving quickly enough, or not wanting class to be boring or too repetitive.

- Do not come into a class defensive of your teaching methods. Be confident that your expectations will help your dancers achieve what they are there for.

- Recognize the lasting benefits of giving your students a strong foundation. Then witness them flourish as independent and hardworking contributors to the dance world.

2

Foundational Constants

Helping dancers maintain their skills

SOME OF THE FIRST codified movements a dancer learns beyond positions of the body are pliés, tendus, dégagés, and relevés. Those steps carry through a dancer's entire training in various forms and adaptations across dance genres. However, I am not referring to those steps as the basics by themselves. The concepts *beneath* those first formative steps are the keys to a strong foundation and building valuable skills in dancers.

All of the basics of technique that we drill in our dancers for years hearken back to the same concepts:

- alignment,

- reaching through the extremities,

- and rotation.

These concepts are at the essence of basic dance movement.

I mentally categorize these specific aspects of technique as **foundational constants.** They are constant because they need to work consistently for dancers to progress. The constants regularly require evaluation and refinement.

We will explore each of these constants more in-depth in their own chapter. Arguably, there are more concepts to focus on as constants in dance, but these are vital concepts that I focus on at the foundation of technique and are applicable across the dance world.

As teachers, we can't merely give dancers a quick plié combination, blast through tendus, give a mind-bending (but messy) dégagé, and call it good. Instead, our students need to do those things correctly while executing the finer details. And if they do them well, the constants behind the steps will create the muscle memory to drive successful dancing.

No matter what level I am teaching, beginners or not, I evaluate these same fundamental aspects of technique in my students. Even when stepping in for another teacher or leading a workshop or audition, I first observe and assess these constants. The constants of basic dance technique tell me a lot about a dancer. They tell me what might be holding them back or what they are ready for next.

When I can help my dancers with their foundational constants, everything else in their technique will more naturally fall into place.

Basic steps solidify the constants

When I think of teaching the basics, the word "maintenance" comes to mind. The only way to maintain healthy teeth and gums is to daily and consistently care for them. I cannot skip brushing my teeth for a year and then go to the dentist and expect him to give me two thumbs up and tell me my mouth looks better than ever! And I cannot make up for lost time and brush for an hour to get ready for my dentist appointment. My mouth would not be conditioned for that, and it would not make up for any long-term effects of not brushing.

The same concept is true for maintaining skill in dancers. I often remind my students that even the principal dancers from the top-performing companies in the world still do their pliés daily. Dancers need to learn, *and continue to work on,* pliés, tendus, and dégagés. They still need to practice stretching and pointing their feet. The foundations of technique do not change–they are only layered upon. Each of those steps builds a foundational aspect of their dance technique.

Pliés are the preparation and grounding for all movements and jumps. But more than that, they can be the perfect workshop to learn about engaging hip rotation and maintaining neutral alignment–both of which must be constant in all movements.

Tendus give a clear lesson in reaching through space from the top of the head and down to the toes. That is the same as the constant of reaching through the extremities.

Dégagés test a dancer's ability to hold rotation for stability and to shift and find balance with various accents and speeds–combining all of the constants.

The list goes on for each of the foundational steps used to warm up the body.

Constants require nuance and repetition

Thinking back to that curriculum meeting with our studio ballet director, she also asked us as teachers to stop any combination and start over if the students weren't executing the movement correctly. This suggestion also made me hesitate. I was worried about wasting time and not getting anywhere. *Can 7-year-olds even do a correct plié, or would I be wasting everyone's time to expect it?* Well, I discovered that, yes, they could do a correct plié! They could, and they would if I required it of them.

Likewise, referencing the basic steps does not equate to low expectations. Basic does not mean "less than" or lacking in substance.

On the contrary, the primary/beginner steps are the building blocks that everything else is layered upon to make fuller technique. Therefore, focusing on the basics of technique means refining the underlying concepts. A robust technical foundation should be an integral part of dance training.

Without requiring the finer details of the foundational constants, we run the risk of our students seeming well-rounded when in actuality, they are becoming mediocre. So rather than sprinkling our students with a glossed-over approach to learning, we should dive deep into those concepts that support all of their dancing.

The constants create a sturdy framework for all of the finer details to build on. If the constants are strong enough, your dancers will not deviate from them when things inevitably become more complex. So, teach nuances with the constants in order for your dancers to learn them thoroughly.

If the nuances aren't there, a plié is just a bend in the legs. Of course, anyone off the street can bend their legs. But mature movement comes from understanding the finer details. Things like musicality, full rotation, proper head position, fully pointed feet, coupled with high demi-pointe, etc., need to be present to turn regular human movement into proper dancing.

And your dancers will rise to the occasion. Do not be afraid to expect precision from even the youngest students. No matter their age or level, dancers can give you those things if you consistently expect them to and give them the appropriate tools to execute them. I have seen many young dancers who can move their heads in unison and have perfect posture and gentle hand shape, all while doing the simplest steps.

It all starts with being consistent with your expectations of the constants of movement. Those things have to be taught early on and unapologetically enforced–then they can be built upon.

We should place quality over quantity. It is more important to do things correctly once instead of drilling them incorrectly several times. Get your dancers to do each step correctly at least one time in each class. Look for consistency in those constant parts of technique.

The constants of technique support all levels

This focus on the basics feels more natural when teaching beginners because you have the opportunity to teach them from the outset. You get to build their technique step by step, brick by brick.

But what if you do not have the luxury of teaching a student from a beginner? You still do not need to apologize for focusing on the basics if needed. Several times, I have had new students who were dancing at an "upper level" at their former studio, and when they come to the studio where I teach, they are more of a middle level based on our standards. Of course, levels are labeled differently everywhere–but the foundations should be present at any level.

Often in those cases, we (as teachers) have to remind those dancers that we have their best interests in mind. We will place them where we think they can have the most success–even if that means taking a step "back" and solidifying more basic movements. And when they are ready, we will not hold them back from advancing levels. The constants lay the foundation for solid dance technique in any setting, regardless of age or level.

The constants are guiding principles that provide the maintenance for solid dancing. And even as our dancers move into steps beyond the basics, we have to make sure the constants are still there supporting them. We won't need to "get back to basics" if we never leave them.

<u>Summary of Chapter Two</u>

- The basics are not just steps that dancers memorize–they are concepts that carry everything they do.

- There are some specific foundations of dance technique that I call the "foundational constants."

- Those constants are alignment, reaching through the extremities, and rotation.

- Teaching nuance with precision and repetition gives dancers a solid base on which to build their technique.

- Even the youngest students can execute the constants well, and it is our job to expect it and require it.

3

Alignment

The first constant

OUR SKELETONS ARE THE scaffolding that supports everything we do. Picture a human skeleton. In a normally developed skeleton, everything is in alignment. There aren't any wonky or crooked hips, pinched shoulders, or splayed ribs. Instead, the bones stack neatly for balance in standing and basic movements like walking. It's functional.

Now, if our skeletons stack so efficiently by design, why do we even need to talk about alignment? Because dancers aim to push their movements to the limits. Their muscles engage and disengage–inevitably affecting natural skeletal alignment.

Dancers are shifting alignment continually, and with that shifting comes a slew of side effects requiring realignment. As teachers, we need to train and discipline ourselves to see those issues in our students and have a way to help them combat that misalignment. Our job is to have the ability to view, diagnose, and find a solution for these issues in our dancers.

Throughout a single dance class, we might observe a number of alignment issues needing correction: hips pitching forward, the torso tilting to either side, the rear sticking out, splayed ribs, shoulders rolled forward or pinched in the back or lifted, etc. The list could go on, and it is overwhelming to correct all of it at once.

But alignment is tied to everything a dancer does; therefore, it requires perpetual evaluation. Ignoring substandard alignment will only breed substandard dancing.

Diagnosing alignment issues using critical checkpoints

A critical checkpoint is a visible indicator for alignment. You can evaluate critical checkpoints to help diagnose and fix your dancer's alignment. These checkpoints are easily seen from the side profile as you walk around and observe your students. Simply look at your dancers' skeletal shape. How do their bones stack and line up? Below are the checkpoints you can observe that affect alignment and weight placement:

First: hip/pelvic placement

It's most helpful to start with pelvic misalignment since it affects alignment up and down the kinetic chain in the torso. For example, if my dancer's rear is swinging back, or if the vertical line of their body has a visible hinge at their hips, I can tell their hips are spilling forward (creating an anterior pelvic tilt). Tilted hips develop problems in a few areas:

- Balance is thrown into the heels. Then balancing on relevé, or even flat-footed, for more than a brief moment is problematic.

- Shortens the body. The torso becomes broken up into several lines going in different directions instead of one vertical or continuous line of energy. This shortening then limits the range of motion. The lumbar spine is compressed and swayed back instead of lengthened.

- Connection to the core support muscles in the abdominals is lost.

Second: rib placement

The ribs are another central indicator in the torso and work in line with the abdominal muscles. They affect the hips down below and the shoulders up above. Open/splayed ribs are a symptom of compromised alignment in a few areas:

- Shoulders pull back. This creates tension or pinching in the shoulder blades and throws the bodyweight backward.

- Shortens the length of the torso. For instance, if the ribs are out of line, it steals length from the vertical line and sends it out the front. This misalignment shortens the body similarly to misalignment in the pelvis.

- Lost connection to the core abdominal muscles.

Third: shoulder placement

Shoulders are placed incorrectly if they are: lifted too high; rolling forward and closed off; or pulling back or pinched. Shoulder misplacement creates problems in a few areas:

- Breeds tension in the upper body. Lifted shoulders come across as tension in the neck. It limits movement and the ability to balance.

- Shortened torso. Lifting the shoulders shortens the neck. Rolling shoulders forward causes slouching. Pinching shoulders either splays the ribs or swings the hips into an anterior pelvic tilt–or a combination of both.

- Shortened range of motion, especially in the arms and upper body.

Notice how many of the alignment issues overlap and cause similar issues. It's hard to know what caused an alignment problem or what was a symptom. While the science of physics makes a lot of dance techniques possible, it can also be subjective at times. Finding what works for specific needs and body types is frequently a process of trial and error.

It is similar to seeing a doctor for an unknown ailment. Your doctor will often give you some suggestions to try to help improve your condition. Sometimes they may ask another doctor or specialist to weigh in. The same concept is accurate for "diagnosing" dancers' alignment issues. We try something and see if it works to improve alignment and reevaluate and redirect as needed.

It's the age-old question, "Which came first, the chicken or the egg?" For instance, shoulder blades pinching in the back could be a symptom of hips swinging back, ribs splaying out in front, or it could be a little bit of both. But squeezing in the shoulders can also *cause* other misalignments. So it's a puzzle to figure out what is initiating the problem.

Again, looking at a human skeleton, the bones stack up to work efficiently, at least when there isn't any interference. To regain neutral alignment, we need to know what is causing that interference.

Chickens

I notice alignment issues in my dancers every class and need to help them adjust constantly. And I have learned that one efficient way to combat a slew of alignment issues is to embody them all and then correct them.

This brings us to the good ol' chicken dance.

A couple of years ago, I experimented with an exercise to help correct some common alignment issues. I told my dancers, who were young beginners, that we would dance like chickens to warm up. I explained my expectations.

Here were the requirements for the chicken dance:

- Students place their hands on their ribs,

- lift their shoulders, and

- stick out their ribs and elbows (as their "chicken wings").

- Then they had to shorten their legs and stick out their rear (for some tail feathers).

Then I asked them to dance around like that. Everything about this alignment is wrong. It was silly and fun and totally wrong. In contrast to the usually rigid structure of dance class, my dancers loved it! We danced around until I told them to freeze in the correct position.

Here were the rules I told them for freezing:

- Feet stop in the first position.

- Close the ribs—zip up the abdominals to bring the pelvis back in line.

- Bring the hands together in the front, and lengthen the arms in the first position.

All of this had to happen in quick succession to hold the position. They quickly went through the checklist: ribs, abdominals, rear/pelvis, lengthen. It's basically a retrograde of all of the misalignment (shown **below**). And I place a focus primarily on how the hips align with everything else above and below.

We did the chicken dance for eight counts, then corrected and held our alignment for eight counts. We did that a few times. Then we did four counts of each. Then 2. Then 1. We also froze in second, third, and fifth position, but the checklist for freezing was still the same. It was like a game to keep up, and it was fun for all of us!

My dancers went from crazy, deformed human birds to beautifully aligned dancers within a minute or two.

It was an experiment, which doubled as a warm-up, and it worked like a charm. The dancers' energy went from silly and chatty to focused and controlled. They quickly found proper alignment and held it each time.

Needless to say, that exercise is now a staple in many of my classes. Even older students can appreciate a version of this exercise by allowing them to practice the contrast of incorrect alignment and quick realignment. It has also worked well with the modern dance classes I have taught.

It was amazing that those young students could take a giant list of alignment issues and fix them in one swoop. That one exercise essentially packed a myriad of corrections into one.

Why does this work?

First, it works because it engages dancers to focus quickly on a checklist of items–which is a constant need in dance.

Next, it gives them a clear contrast of what doesn't work and immediately follows up with what works.

Finally, an exercise like this is memorable. It leaves more of an impact than just saying the words "pull in your ribs and realign the hips." And having them hold correct alignment for a few counts also helped them solidify that feeling.

Another exercise that I often use with other classes (older or adult students who aren't as interested in dancing around like chickens) achieves similar results. Like the chicken dance, we use it as a warm-up to get everything aligned for class. I call it the spine roll-through exercise. Here's how this exercise goes:

I have the dancers face the barre and stand back far enough to hold the barre and fully extend the back as they bend forward. The cues are similar to the chicken dance: extend the rear back, shorten the neck, stick out the ribs, and shoot the belly forward (**first image**).

Then I have them drop their head (**second image**) and slowly "zip" their abdominals back together in the front–re-stacking all the vertebrae in the spine (**third image**). I have the dancers finish by dropping their shoulders back into place at the top (**fourth image**). It gently warms up the mobility in the spine and hamstrings and aligns the hips and torso easily and beautifully.

After a few repetitions, I have them step into the barre and finish the combination with their newly engaged neutral alignment. This exercise also translates well into contemporary and modern technique classes.

Another benefit of exercises like the spine roll-through exercise and the chicken dance is that when my dancers struggled with alignment, we could easily recall the helpful concepts of those exercises. Exercises like these are impactful because they engage dancers in finding alignment on their own. All it took to engross them was exaggerated and fun misalignment, fixing it, and repeating. Then I could ask my dancers to soften their ribs and realign their hips, and they knew what I was talking about. (We will discuss more ways to engage dancers in Chapter 8.)

Correcting alignment one time in class is not enough. My friend and colleague Corinne uses the phrase "evident and enduring" in relation to foundational concepts–specifically including alignment. It needs continuous attention and refining to endure through the rigors of dance training. **So, if you can address one thing to begin class, spend a minute or two on the alignment of the hips.**

Even if you forgo exercises like the ones I mentioned, at the very least take the time at the beginning of class to have your dancers find neutral pelvic alignment. Have them practice tilting/spilling their hips forward and then zipping up their abdominals in the front and lengthening their lumbar spine to realign. Neutral pelvic alignment is also invaluable for contemporary and modern dance movements that push the limits of balance and spinal flexibility. Dancers will always need the skill to return to the stability of neutral alignment.

Accordions

Every one of the alignment problems we've covered has something in common–shortening. We discovered that in our discussion on critical checkpoints earlier in this chapter. Misalignment in the hips, ribs, or shoulders shortens the length of the torso to some degree. Shortened movement is never what we want our dancers to strive for.

However, if you simply tell a dancer to "lift up" or "stand taller," you may notice other problems creeping in. Just saying "lift up" causes many dancers to lose the grounding and downward energy in their shoulders (or not engaging their latissimus dorsi). As a result, their neck can become short and tense. The upward tension can even throw them back. This is part of the reason you may see dancers falling backward in their turns when they try to lift while turning. In addition, dancers will often lose their grounding on the floor when they pull back.

I was thinking a lot about this a few years ago and wanted a way to help correct alignment and avoid shortening the body. I was cueing my dancers with those exact phrases we often use as teachers: "Lift up!" "Stand tall!". The verbal corrections could only go so far, though. My students needed a visual to help embody the way to lift correctly.

Then, among my son's toys, I found a visual that worked to help with understanding this aspect of alignment. This is the accordion baby toy my students affectionately named Zeke the Zebra.

After doing the chicken dance, I introduced my little accordion zebra. We used the same checklist when we froze in our positions (ribs, abdominals, rear, lengthen), but I showed them how to elongate their bodies like an accordion in addition to aligning their torsos.

It helped to point out the contrast. I demonstrated a slouched and shortened body to the dancers versus an elongated and lifted one. I had them do it with me as I compressed and extended the accordion. I pointed out that it was growing and lengthening upward, but it was also extending downward. Their bodies would easily imitate lengthening their torso as I stretched out the accordion. The visual helped something click for them mentally and physically. They could picture their spine stretching and creating space similar to the ribbed visual of an accordion.

Reminding them to close their ribs before lifting up/lengthening was also critical. This reminder prevented them from falling backward as they lifted.

Another key to this concept is to have my dancers picture more than one accordion in their bodies. So I have them imagine vertical accordions in their torso and neck and another horizontal accordion stretching through the width of their shoulders.

This imagery immediately helps the dancers drop their shoulders back where they need to be. They can also picture an accordion in their elbows, lengthening their arms out into the open space. The accordion imagery also works well for extending the ankles when pointing the feet and in the knees when looking for straight legs.

It's a valuable and quick visual tool. And Zeke has become somewhat of a dance class mascot.

It's also a helpful image for those dancers who tend to try "too hard" and hold a lot of unnecessary tension. I know this because growing up, I was often that dancer. I often found myself straining and stiff because I tried so hard to hold all of my muscles to achieve perfect technique. And dancing so rigidly shortened my movement. Lengthening in the proper alignment helps those particularly tense dancers begin working smarter–not necessarily harder.

Lifting within the confines of appropriate alignment frees up the body to function the way it is made to.

The accordion imagery itself is not the specific takeaway here. Dancers need all kinds of visuals and reminders. Dancers understand the constants of movement in more ways than just one-word corrections that we shout above our class music. But we must put in the effort to make proper alignment real and achievable for our dancers.

Finding alignment, then, needs to continue over and over. Train your dancers to go through the process of finding their alignment again and again going through a checklist after they inevitably leave it. They will eventually move beyond simple positions and steps and into more intricate movements. And with each advancement, make sure they continue to go back to their neutral alignment as their foundation and constant.

For example, after their hips move and tilt to make arabesque happen, train your dancers to realign and lift up and forward as they close the leg. After they open their chest and stretch back for cambré derrière, teach them to realign the ribs and lift in the abdominals as they return to standing. After they push the boundaries of balance and center alignment in modern and contemporary styles, have them find alignment once more. Again and again, realign and lengthen.

If you lay the alignment foundation often, with time, your dancers will start to find it on their own with more speed and exactness.

Solidifying neutral pelvic alignment is just the beginning though. Another major part of alignment is finding the centerline of the body in order to balance during the inevitable shifts in alignment.

Utilizing proper alignment for balance

Dance is movement. Stagnant positions are few and far between. And any action when a dancer has incorrect center alignment closes the door on free, and seemingly effortless movement–poor weight placement instills a fight against the laws of physics. That is why knowledge of alignment and balance go hand in hand.

A consistent ability to balance is an alignment issue. It's not solely a natural ability, nor is it limited to specific body types.

Thinking back to my years of dancing, I don't know if I understood how to use my alignment to balance more efficiently until I was an adult. It just seemed like some dancers had the "it factor" for balance, and everyone else was just out of luck. Some days I felt like I had it, and on others, I didn't. It was hard to tell what made the difference. It was frustrating to think that I had little control over my ability to balance and control the descent of my limbs after they left the ground.

Dancers need lessons on where they should center their alignment in order to balance. They need to learn to realign their weight placement each time they move. Their balance must shift as soon as they move away from a symmetrical or preparatory pose. Even in a seemingly stagnant position, dancers should feel that their weight is actively reaching up and forward. And even young dancers can learn to have control over their movement and ability to balance. They should not dance for years without this knowledge, only to learn later on that they just needed to shift their weight every time they moved.

As their teacher, take the time to break down each movement and *teach* your students where they should be shifting their weight. You can positively affect your students' ability to balance when you address their hips and arms.

Hips

Shifting weight has to happen at the hips/pelvis without losing attachment to the core abdominal muscles. In other words, we can't just tell our dancers to move their hips for better balance. The hips are a central indicator of alignment, but they can't lose their connection to the rest of the body.

For example, in something as basic as a tendu, I explain to my students to lift up and over the standing leg. Then, I show it to them. If they perform a tendu á la seconde with the right foot, their body should shift up and over to the left. The same is true for derrière movements. If the leg needs to extend back (especially en l'air), the alignment must shift forward and lift to make space for the leg below.

But shifting over the standing leg doesn't mean leaning the upper body away from the tendu. On the contrary, leaning can cause a pelvic lift/tilt and possibly exacerbates the issue of uneven hips (shown across in the **first image**). So instead, the hips themselves have to move ever so slightly and adjust to the standing leg (**second image**).

Eric Franklin, the creator of the Franklin Method of movement, mentions this very thing in his book *Dance Imagery for Technique and Performance.* He explains that the best way to improve balancing alignment is to strengthen coordination first. He calls it the "alignment paradox"[2] when we have to move another part of our body to counterbalance and maintain a center of gravity.

We have to teach our dancers to coordinate their movement with the counterbalancing movement to maintain balance. When dancers discover this idea and lift each time they shift, they will find the freedom to balance in their tendu and even raise their leg freely. Proper alignment and weight placement then become easier and more efficient.

Have your dancers test it out. First, tendu in any direction and try to lift the toe. If they cannot raise their toe off the floor without it slamming back down, they need to realign their hips in relation to their weight placement. Incorporating the accordion imagery for alignment will often fix this problem. But if a dancer needs additional help, they can gently shift their hips (aligned with their upper body) away from that extended leg. Then they will immediately find more freedom in their balance.

It's like magic! But it's more like physics. And it is achievable for anyone with a bit of attention to detail. Dancers just have to know the details to look for and practice. And as their teacher, you open up that realization and that "ah-ha" moment for them.

Arms

Arm placement drastically impacts bodyweight alignment and balance as well. You can see it easily when your students put their hand on the barre or with their arms extended in second position out on the center floor.

Next time you are teaching, look at your dancers holding the barre. I am not referring to their grip. Dancers often get the reminder to avoid the "death grip" on the barre. That is often just a side effect of not being able to balance autonomously or holding unnecessary tension in the body, which we aim to fix with proper focus.

Instead, look at the length of your dancers' arms and where their elbows are. If their arm is short, or their elbow is jutting out behind them, there needs to be some adjustment. And yes, the arms are allowed in the back space in some movements in dance. But dancers can only move into that space once they understand the needed connection to their core and alignment.

Many well-meaning teachers simply walk around and adjust arm placement at the barre without a word. I have done this as I make my rounds around the studio during an exercise. But instead of just changing where your dancers place their arms, offer a brief explanation of why.

Point out your dancer's short arm at the barre. Explain that with their elbow behind them, it can pull them backward, lift their shoulder, and can even splay their ribs. It also engrains in their muscle memory how to dance without fully extended arms.

If your dancers can see how a shortened arm at the barre translates to a shortened arm in the center, they can see why we don't hold the barre so closely. Have them walk away from the barre and keep their arm in the same shortened shape. It looks like a clipped chicken wing, just like the chicken dance! It can throw off the alignment and limit the range of motion–affecting their reach through the extremities.

Now remind them that lengthening their arm into the forward space at the barre, or stepping slightly away from the barre, gives them more freedom in movement and allows their weight to adjust to balance each time they move (**demonstrated below**).

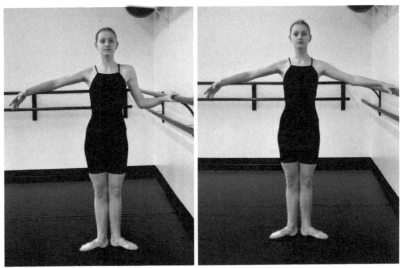

shortened arm vs. lengthened arm

I have found that if I tell my dancers why I am adjusting their arms, they are more likely to recognize the need for better placement. As a result, the correction is more likely to stick and they will correct themselves autonomously.

One additional note

I have used the word "weight" several times in this chapter. Obviously, I am not talking about a student's weight on the scale. Weight placement has nothing to do with the size or shape of your students. Instead, weight placement refers to the physics of aligning different parts of the body. Proper weight placement allows for more balance with less effort.

Addressing your students' weight can breed an unhealthy body image. I will briefly address the issue of talking about "weight" with your dancers in Chapter 11.

<u>Summary of Chapter Three</u>

- Most misalignment issues happen in the hips, ribs, and shoulders - checkpoints you can easily evaluate by looking at your dancers' skeletal profile.

- Learning to realign and lengthen up and forward frequently will help dancers to eventually fix misalignment autonomously and gain control of their dancing.

- The pelvis is the center of the body and the center of every movement in the body.

- Pelvic alignment goes hand in hand with balance.

- Balance is a learned skill, not the luck of the draw. Addressing the placement of the hips and arms in coordination with alignment will improve balance.

- Once you teach your dancers the concepts and the coordination, require it again and again.

4

Reaching Through the Extremities

The second constant

TRY A SIMPLE EXPERIMENT. Grab a dry erase marker and stand next to a mirror. If you fully extend your arm and make a circle motion with your arm, you will be able to draw a near-perfect circle on the mirror. (You can even try this with your dancers.) Similarly, if you could dip your toe in paint and fully extend your leg, you can trace a flawless half-circle with your toe on the floor. It's fun to see the perfection in something so simple.

The human body is full of natural and appealing circular and linear patterns–which dancers can create if they simply elongate fully through their extremities. That's one reason why dance is so intriguing and enjoyable to watch. It naturally and subconsciously draws in the audience. Dancers need to learn to use their reach through space.

But learning to use a full range of motion is not something to teach dancers after the fact. It is not a switch to turn on just in time for a performance. Reaching is a constant. It's foundational to functional and whole movement.

Dancers who learn only to dance small will have a more challenging time dancing "full out" when it is asked of them. So, require full movement in your dancers from the beginning–then the muscle memory can be there. It's not just the cherry on top, but a guiding force to dancing completely and artistically.

You can begin teaching this constant by helping your dancers identify when they have performed steps with full extension, and those naturally aesthetic circles and lines are apparent. For example, students can easily see and feel natural circles in the body while doing movements that are innately circular: rond de jambe á terre and en l'air, grand battement, port de bras, etc.

Then you can help your students find that same extension in more complicated movements when the pathways for reaching are not so straightforward. For instance, a fouetté turn has an extension with the rond, but it also comes into a retíre position. You could remind your dancers to find that full extension with each repetition and to keep the torso fully extended vertically when coming into the "shorter" retíre position. They can find reach in their retíre as well when they think of expanding their width side to side.

Reaching is functional

In my mind, the concept of reaching is more than just stretching the limbs and fingers and toes to their full extent. It is dancing "full out" in even the nuanced aspects. Using the extremities has a purpose beyond aesthetics, artistry and filling up space on a stage. Reaching to the edges of a dancer's personal space also adds to the movement's function. Reaching can actually make some steps easier to execute.

Sometimes when I teach pirouettes (or other turns like piqués and chaînés), I demonstrate the analogy of the pen versus the spinning top. It's an excellent way to show how reaching should be multidirectional for it to simplify the function of turning. There are opposing forces to make it work.

If you take a pen, stand it up on the tip, and try to spin it, you might get half a spin before the pen falls over. Of course, a pen *is* tall and long, but that alone won't make it balanced.

Contrastingly, if you look at the shape of a spinning top, you still see a fine point at the bottom and a vertical centerline. But in addition, a spinning top has a wide middle reaching out around the whole centerline. It balances while spinning because it combines a lifted centerline and an expanding opposing force out the sides.

The same is valid for balance while turning.

A basic pirouette works the best when dancers reach wide and long through all extremities. The center of the body should be tall and lengthened. The arms should reach long in the front and wide and open at the elbows, shoulders, and back. The knee should be opened wide in the retíre position. The opposing forces (up and down, side to side) are what allow the dancer to continue turning without falling over. Multiple rotations are only possible when the body reaches and lifts in all directions.

Multidirectional reaching adds to the function and dynamics of arabesque as well. In arabesque, the dancer extends their leg behind them while *also* adjusting the torso to make room in the back. That forward reach in the chest and arms creates an opposing force to counterbalance the leg in arabesque. Reaching forward opens space for the leg to move more freely and openly.

When my students finally put this concept together, they are often caught off guard by the newfound balance and openness they feel at the top of their turn or in their arabesque. If reaching wide is combined with the concept of alignment, their hips are in place to hold the balance. It's freeing to realize that turning is something they can figure out with their own bodies. It doesn't seem as difficult anymore.

Reaching through the extremities is functional in many movements–pirouette in retiré is just one example. A basic sauté has more hang time and power only when dancers propel their jump with their entire feet and toes. A grand plié turns into just a squat without reaching and lifting out of the legs to maintain control. Leaping covers more ground when the working leg reaches full extension and is accompanied by a complete extension from the back leg. Something as small as rising to demi-pointe still requires thorough extension and stretching through the legs to be stable and maintain balance. A tombé is just a slam if not coupled with a preceding reach and lift.

The list could go on. Our dancers only benefit if we teach them this concept from the beginning of their training, and they lack stability and even safety without it. Movements and positions that are executed half-heartedly are weaker and more susceptible to injury. Evaluate, correct, and reinforce the need for your dancers to utilize their extremities.

Stretching is an action, not a placement

Calling this second constant "reaching through the extremities" is an oversimplification. It is more than fully incorporating the limbs. It is dancing broadly with quality and intention and whole-body movement from the inside and out. It is nuances as small as a purposeful inclination of the head. It is dancing with artistry.

Using a full range of motion applies to many aspects of the body, but frequently the extremities are left out–the tips of the fingers, tips of the toes, and the gaze of the eyes. The extremities often become an afterthought that we address only when "cleaning" up movement. We don't usually give them enough individual focus from the movement's inception. Feet need their own warm-up and attention to detail throughout the class. The extension and shape of the hands and fingers need special attention. From the top of the head and down through the torso, dancers should be learning to reach those extremities, and they will find more ease and fullness in their movement.

One analogy that helps my students find their extremities is to picture a dog or cat taking an afternoon nap on the rug in the sun's warmth streaming through the window. When they wake up from their naps, it is a slow and almost deliberate awakening of every part of their bodies. You can see the cat reaching through her spine and all the way through her tail. You can picture the dog stretching its front paws as far as possible and releasing a giant yawn.

In dance, that is the action of tendu.

A pointed foot is not just a place of arrival. It is the product of reaching and stretching.

Whenever I teach tendus (the first awakenings of a pointed foot in class), I explain that tendu means to stretch. So, tendu is everything leading up to the pointed toes at the end and should come from the top of the head. Then it is energy going through the torso, down the leg, and finally out the extended foot to the tips of the toes.

Stretching is an action, not a placement. I often ask my dancers to imagine themselves stretching after a long nap and ask them to practice their own big yawn and stretch, then keep that idea in mind as they tendu.

If dancers can grasp the concept of reaching their extremities, their artistry can have no limits and basic movements like tendu become full and complete. They can use their body to their full range of motion and artistic potential. Again, it's the concept of following through and committing to the movement to the very tips and edges.

If you look at a person shooting a basketball in slow motion, you can see the embodiment of follow-through. They extend their arms from their body and release the ball from their fingers to propel the ball in the right direction. The push continues like a wave through their hands until their wrists complete the follow-through.

As dancers, our feet and hands can have that same follow-through. Teach your students to commit to that follow-through. It will not happen unless you require it and consistently correct it.

We know that their endurance and muscle memory will begin to take the lead if we require the finer details constantly from the outset. So, why would we let our dancers practice incorrectly? Correct your dancers if they are wrong, and start again. So when you focus on this constant, don't allow improper foot shapes like sickling or winging or stiff or misshapen hands. We want to correct the nuances that make the technique more complete.

Tips for teaching a reach in the extremities: arms

Recall the discussion about how lengthening the arms (even at the barre) helps with weight placement and balance? Shortened arms take away from functional dancing and prepare dancers for constricted movement. Yet, it is difficult for students to find and maintain a reach in a stagnant position like holding onto the barre or holding the arms wide in the second position.

Here is a set of cues that have helped my dancers find a powerful and reaching second position with their arms–which then carries over into reaching in the upper body through additional movements. I am not sure who is the originator of this tip, but it is invaluable for teaching a proper second position (shown on the following page):

1. Face straight forward and reach both arms to the side with shoulders down and chest open. Flex hands and send energy out the palms. This position is the proper placement of the **shoulders**.

2. While keeping that shoulder placement, next rotate both flexed hands forward. Avoid closing off the chest or rolling the shoulders in. This position is the placement of the **elbows** in a proper second position.

3. While maintaining the placement of the shoulders and elbows, then rotate the forearms and the wrists to turn the palms of the **hands** to face the body. This position is a properly reaching second position.

If your dancers' arms are shriveling, this is a great exercise to remedy that.

This practice can be applied to finding a true high fifth position by following the same outline. **First**, reach the arms straight above the head with the palms facing up toward the ceiling, and drop the shoulders. **Next**, turn the flexed palms so the fingertips are pointing at each other. This is the placement of the elbows in the high fifth. **Finally**, rotate the hands from the wrists until the palms are facing the body instead of the ceiling. This is a clean high fifth position.

Important note for both port de bras practices: The final step of rotating the wrists, so the palms fully face the body is crucial. Often, the reason the arms look droopy or "dead" is that missing torque in the forearms which completes the aesthetic lines in basic port de bras positions.

Tips for teaching a reach in the extremities: feet

Finding a complete reach through the toes is attainable through the formative steps like tendus and rond de jambes. The reaching is built-in with the idea of finding those natural linear and circular patterns of the body. And it is simple to maintain that extension at slower speeds. However, dancers can easily lose their reaching toes when they move on to jumps and faster movements.

If my dancers are struggling to use their feet in jumps, I have found one exercise, in particular, to be helpful in compelling dancers to reach with their feet and toes thoroughly (visual on the next page):

1. Stand in first position with the feet. Place the arms either in a reaching second or on the hips. (**first image**)

2. While lifting up and forward, press the legs together and the feet down into the floor.

3. Press down with enough power in the feet to propel upwards into a shallow "jump" without a preceding plié. The height of the jump is not the most critical aspect here. Place the importance on using the entire foot through the toes. (**second image**)

4. Slow the descent by coming through demi-pointe and resisting the urge to "plop" down quickly–it helps to imagine something like the sensation of squashing oranges under the heels or thinking of reaching up while coming down. (**third image**)

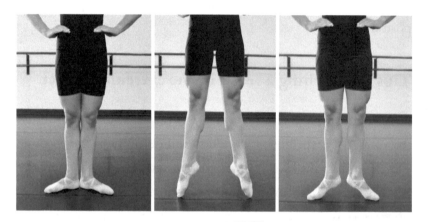

This exercise is a challenge for most dancers, but it forces the use of the metatarsals and intrinsic muscles of the feet. I usually have my dancers do this exercise slowly–starting with 8 repetitions. Then we build up to more repetitions and greater speed over time to train using the extremities during quicker movements.

If your dancers can maintain rotation and a relaxed upper body, they can try this exercise. Their first "jumps" may not even leave the floor, but over time they will gain the strength in their feet to leave the ground. Then adding a plié will be the finishing touch to jumping with full use of the extremities in the feet. Though, younger dancers might benefit from "jumping off the wall" and propelling their bodies along the floor in a seated position and finishing with lifted torsos, stretched legs, and pointed toes. Both exercises work well as a practice in stretching the feet to the extremities.

Summary of Chapter Four

- Reaching through the extremities is not only correct aesthetically, but serves a functional purpose.

- Fully extended lines coupled with correct alignment promote balance and stability.

- Dance teachers should specifically teach the concept of reaching through the extremities and evaluate it often since alignment is shifting constantly with dance movement.

- Dancers who extend their energy out past their extremities will find they can simultaneously cover more space and feel more grounded on the floor.

- Helping our dancers understand how to use their extremities properly will result in them dancing more broadly and more functionally–adding maturity to their dancing.

5

Rotation

The third constant

PICTURE A WELL-LOVED, DUSTY old book. If you lay it open to the center page, the cracked binding will allow the pages to rest open gently–equal pages on each side. It is freely opening from the center and not squeezing, but simply pressing down and open.

In dance, this is the feeling of proper rotation. It's not a result of squeezing the glutes as hard as possible. It is not forced by planting the feet firmly to the ground and holding them there. Instead, it is a gentle and firm rotation of both legs entirely.

Thoughts on ideal rotation

The ideal rotation amount can be a controversial subject, particularly in ballet. My position is that a dancer doesn't need to have a specific amount of turnout. The benefits of engaging and maintaining the rotator muscles extend beyond an aesthetic. Any genre of dance that requires strength and stability in the supporting leg(s) uses the same skills found in the primary rotation techniques. Proper rotation creates a sleeve of muscular stability–wrapping around the leg and giving it strength.

I think rotation, or turnout, is subjective and malleable. I am a firm believer in finding and maximizing natural turnout instead of fabricating a 180-degree first position in the feet.

We should not expect our dancers to work up to that supposed "perfect" rotation to find any success. And thankfully, I see a movement away from that school of thought. Instead, it seems that directors and companies are becoming more accepting that perfect rotation does not make the dancer great.

A broad range of motion is vital in dance. And when dancers work with their entire personal rotation, they are more free to dance than when they sacrifice proper placement for "perfect" rotation.

Students' rotation can also improve the more they work on it. Practicing to improve my rotation was true for me as a dancer, and I have seen it with students time and again. Some students naturally have minimal rotational ability and should not force it. Instead, they can work and find that their rotation is malleable and can improve over time to an extent.

Do not shame a student for not reaching a predetermined turnout cutoff that you have set. For example, I do not want to tell my dancers that a 180-degree turnout is the goal. If that was the goal, I would fail the majority of my students by pushing their limits of rotation to the point of injury. We don't want our dancers to think that an inability to attain that specific rotation means that dancing is not for them.

Rotation is still a constant, though—even though the level of rotational ability in the hips will be different for everyone. It's not essential because dancers need a certain amount of it. It's important because of the strength and muscle awareness that comes with proper rotation. It's not just for ballet technique, but for stability in all forms of dance training. I love what Gretchen Ward Warren says about this in her book *Classical Ballet Technique.* She says, "very few human bodies possess the capacity for perfect turn-out. [A students'] goal must be to develop the muscular strength to control and maintain their own maximum degree of turn-out at all times while they are dancing."[3]

Proper engagement of the rotators places the legs in a safe and robust place. Rotational engagement creates stability within the hips above, supports the knees in alignment below, and opens up the hips to a broader range of motion. In no way is rotation solely for aesthetics. The functions of rotational awareness outweigh the emphasis on visually perfect rotation.

Finding proper rotation

The goal is full *personal* rotation. I quickly correct it if I find my students forcing or adjusting their feet to a 180-degree first position. I do not go around the studio and externally adjust my dancers' feet into that position either. Promoting safety and longevity is essential, and a forced rotation doesn't help either.

Rotation is affected dramatically by the first constant: alignment (as are many things.) A dancer with tilted, or tucked hips, cannot use their natural and full rotation. Full rotation in the hips can only work if the dancer's pelvis is aligned. It all works together. It's physics.

Don't look at a dancer's foot rotation to assess hip rotation. Don't train your dancers to look to their feet for an accurate measure of their rotation, either.

I remember as a young dancer that there was a particular studio that my peers and I complained about because the flooring was made of wood. It was slick, and we all felt like it was a challenge to place our feet in a rotated position and keep them there. So we preferred the Marley (vinyl) floors because we could plant our feet in our desired rotation and keep them there. I didn't understand until later in my training that planting my feet on the floor was not necessarily a good measure of my ability to rotate in my hips. (In retrospect, that wood floor was better for me to build rotational strength because I had to fight to maintain it.)

There are several measures of a dancer's rotation before focusing on the feet. Instead, train your dancers to focus on specific aspects of their dancing that positively impact their rotation.

I observe my dancers' alignment at certain critical checkpoints to help with rotation. And when the time calls for it, I take the time to discuss these and explore them as a class.

Checkpoint 1: Pelvis

Watch for a tilted (anterior) or tucked pelvis (posterior tilt). Either of those would limit full rotation. We discussed the necessity of pelvic alignment previously, but it helps to view it in conjunction with rotation. When everything is aligned, the legs have more space within the hips to move in their complete range of motion–which means full rotation and muscular engagement in the legs.

One cue that has worked for my dancers is the image of a toaster. Here's how we discuss this image: Imagine you are a giant piece of bread inside of an upright toaster. You can go down and up (plié), but you get burnt if you tilt forward or backward! Tilting the pelvis and sticking out the rear or leaning forward with the chest will make burnt edges of toast. Try to plié up and down without burning your toast.

This imagery produces proper vertical alignment that doesn't interfere with rotation. If my dancers are aligned correctly in their pelvis/torso, I move to checkpoint 2.

Checkpoint 2: Knees

I look at their knees and observe which direction they are pointing. Pointing forward shows me they are not using their best rotation. I want to see their knees rotated to the side–which is easiest to find in plié.

Proper rotation can, in fact, *initiate* plié. For example, if you have your dancers move slowly enough and ask them to work on reaching their knees over their pinky toes, they will automatically begin to plié in full rotation.

Especially when inexperienced dancers plié, their knees can point in all sorts of directions. They need to be trained and reminded to track their knees over their pinky toes.

To help my younger dancers remember these things, I like to use the phrase "practically perfect pliés point over pinky toes." That's it. It's simple but formative to technique. If the hips are in line and the knees are opening and reaching back, their rotation is at work in the best way.

Another helpful idea for rotation is the brick wall imagery when thinking about the knees. Have your dancers envision a brick wall directly in front of their face and directly behind their back. Then, as they perform a simple plié, their knees do not want to brush up against the brick walls. Instead, they need to reach over the pinky toes to avoid scraping. It's similar to the toaster idea.

Then I move down the body to checkpoint 3.

Checkpoint 3: Arches

At the bottom, I watch the arches of my dancers' feet as they move. I look for the balance between the medial arch and the outside edge of their foot.

If their weight is centered in their feet, that indicates that my dancers are rotating without compromising anything. Conversely, rolling in or collapsing the arches shows me they might be overcompensating in their feet for lack of rotation or proper alignment above.

To check for this, make sure your dancers keep all of their toes evenly on the floor. This includes their pinky toes, which shouldn't be difficult to remember since they've already been thinking about plié-ing over them. You can also remind dancers to leave their arch open—like a little cave for a tiny creature or a turtle shell. They should not collapse the entrance to the cave or crush the shell. Your dancers will then have safer alignment with their knees and a broader range of motion and depth to their movement. This kind of adjustment is acute and so small but makes a difference.

The pictures across illustrate the contrast. The **first image** is collapsing the arches and rolling the feet forward. The pinky toes are off the ground. The knees are torqued in—not aligning with the rest of the leg. The **second image** shows the corrected alignment of the knees with all toes on the floor, and the knees safely lined up over the toes.

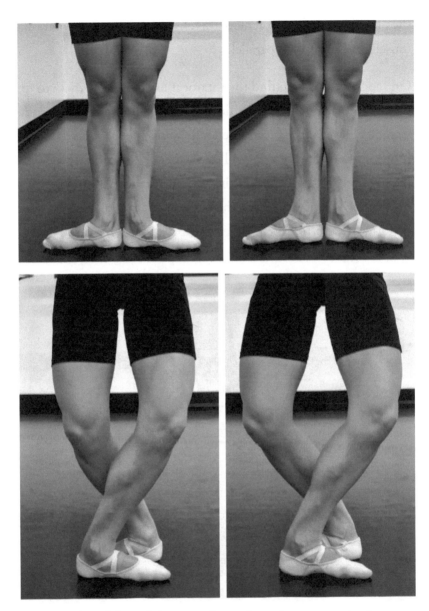

The **third and fourth images** above show the contrast in the range of motion with a plié. Rolled in arches and knees=limited range of motion vs. fully rotated and aligned=more extensive range of motion. This same concept applies in parallel positions. The knees should track in line with the center of the feet and not wing to either the outside or inside. To achieve this alignment, the same rotational muscles are engaged in parallel.

One additional way to find the rotator muscles and get them to fire up is in a sitting straddle. Sit down on the floor with the legs in a straddle. Have your dancers stretch forward. Inexperienced dancers (not engaging their rotators) will allow their legs to roll forward with the stretch. To avoid the rolling in, and engage the rotators, have your dancers fully flex their feet (eel their knees pull up as they engage their quadriceps) and roll their pinky toes back (**demonstrated in the following photos**).

When I first teach young students how to stretch, we explore this. We sometimes imagine making a pizza (or cookie, rolls, etc.), and they are rolling out the dough in front of them as they straddle–a common practice in beginner dance classes. Then, as they reach farther forward to stretch, I remind them to lift their toes (flex) and pull their toes out of their dough (rotate back)–because no one wants toes in their food! It works. They will naturally engage their rotators. It's funny how such a simple cue can work.

Additionally, the glutes will not take over as the primary rotators in this straddle position. So this is a good exercise for students having difficulty separating the sensation of using their glutes instead of their rotators as the main drivers to turnout. The feet will not sickle in this position, and the stretch is more efficient.

You can even take this into further applications and have your dancers keep their legs rotated outward as they slowly bring them forward to a first position. This variation of the exercise can translate more easily to standing positions.

Rotator muscles are smaller than the glutes, but even younger and newer dancers can find them. Being aware of the rotators is not unattainable. We can help our dancers find those harder-to-engage muscles.

Putting it all together and maintaining rotation

Rotation is not necessary for all types of dance all the time, but the muscles and rotational awareness are essential for any sort of stability. They create a dynamic sleeve of muscles encircling the leg and stabilizing at the insertion into the hip. This stability is especially crucial on one leg or in off-balance contemporary movements. Proper use of rotation is also *imperative* for pointe work in ballet training. (I address pointe work separately in Chapter 6.)

The checkpoints of rotation (hips, knees, feet) can be observed quickly and adjusted just as quickly. I have noticed that correcting all of these checkpoints helps get my dancers using their full personal rotation.

I have had many "ah-ha!" moments in class when students realized that one of those checkpoints was off and holding them back. And as soon as they correct it, they feel a sense of accomplishment and see progress moving forward.

Improvement in dance technique becomes more accessible when we aren't fighting our body alignment.

In the beginning steps and positions, the checkpoints at the hips, knees, and feet are easy to assess. Then, consider your dancers' rotation again as soon as they start moving more and lifting their legs off the floor. Have them go through the checklist with you. Quicker and larger movements are the most likely culprits to losing rotation, so it needs to be reassessed when you add those movements to classwork.

For example: if students are lifting á la seconde and their hip is lifting out of alignment, help them drop the hip to realign the pelvis and bring the leg forward slightly to find their rotation again. Make their movements or extensions smaller until they find their rotation. Then they can start to pull the leg more directly to the side once they have found the correct hip placement. The same is valid for speed. If a faster pace is causing your dancers to lose their critical checkpoints of rotation, slow things down until they can solidify that feeling.

It's exciting when dancers piece it together and realize that hard work in dance doesn't have to feel so physically tricky. It is just as much a mental effort as a physical effort to ask dancers to go through the checklists you set out for them. There is a difference between intelligent dancers and those who need direction in every little thing. Dancers with a higher "dance IQ" can make those connections. Yes, their muscles will feel the work, but they will have more endurance and longevity with this approach to learning.

One additional note

I don't cue my dancers to squeeze their glutes—they contribute little to maintaining control in the ball and socket joint in the hips. Squeezing those muscles might make your dancers feel like they are working harder, but it's not accomplishing increased rotation. It's just adding work and limiting movement. Instead, teach them to find more internal rotator muscles.

<u>**Summary of Chapter Five**</u>

- Dancers find their hip rotation on an individual basis.

- Rather than moving your dancers' feet to see "ideal" rotation, teach them to go through a checklist and evaluate and push the limits of their rotation/turnout from the top down to the feet.

- Evaluate hip placement, knee direction, and balance between the arches and the back of the feet.

- Proper rotational engagement will provide more range of motion and safety in movement in ballet technique and other genres of dance.

- Personal rotation can even improve over time by pushing to the bounds within the appropriate placement.

6

Etiquette, Attitude, and Details

The nuances

BEYOND THE SPECIFIC TECHNICAL constants of alignment, lengthening, and rotation, I will not stray far from a couple of other things with my students. Dance teachers can focus on many nitty-gritty details, but I will address:

- warming up,

- professionalism,

- musicality,

- and pointe work.

These are the things that help build a professional culture in the studio–a culture that allows dancers to build up a healthy respect for you as their teacher and the environment around them.

You can set the tone for how your dancers approach their training. How will a student learn to hold their head or have soft hands if they have never practiced, or only practiced incorrectly, for years? How will a student become attentive to musicality if they are never required to stretch their movement to span the length of the music? If you build these expectations of the nuances into your teaching, your dancers will better understand the effort, dedication, and professionalism dance requires.

Warm-up and stretching

It is easy for dancers to get together and jump straight into showing off their super splits, backbends, and other extreme stretches. I have often walked into auditions and workshops only to see dancers contorted as they stretch before class. Seeing this always makes me a little uncomfortable because I know the body only lasts as long as we take care of it.

Stretching isn't a wrong thing to do. Of course, dancers need a certain level of flexibility, and they need to work on it continually. But dancers skip warming up when they pop into their splits as soon as they get into the studio.

Maybe those dancers don't know the importance of a proper warm-up. Perhaps they are imitating what they see online in highlight videos and extreme displays of flexibility on social media. Either way, it is not sustainable in real life. We want our students to value taking care of their bodies. Preparing the body for dance is important, actually vital, to safe dancing and longevity.

Be sure to stress the importance of always warming up first to your dancers. In *A Handbook for the Ballet Accompanist*, it states, "The work at barre serves to warm up the dancer's muscles gradually and systematically, while toning and training them [...] Proper work in the center is not possible unless the dancer works properly at the barre. Any faults or flaws in the [warm up] will be exposed and magnified in the center."[4] This is valid for all dance forms–not just those that begin at the barre. The concept holds true: warming up is essential to lasting success in dance.

I have heard the phrase before that dancing only lasts a while, but the body is forever. So teach your dancers to take care of their bodies, and it will serve them well and for much longer.

I have found that improving flexibility is best focused on at the end of class. When dancers are entirely warmed up, you can use that time to improve flexibility and spend time stretching. Stretching in each class is valuable. We just need to make sure our dancers are doing it effectively, safely, and at the appropriate time. It is much more effective to perform dynamic stretching when dancers are fully warmed up. Static stretching and stretching without a proper warm-up will not breed increased flexibility.

Another aspect of warming up is finding the appropriate muscles intentionally and slowly. For example, besides flexibility, dancers also need awareness in their core abdominals (which helps engage neutral alignment–the first constant). However, warming up with a bunch of crunches and sit-ups and trying to get in numerous quick repetitions is not the best way to awaken those muscles for the remainder of the class. Abdominal warm-ups and exercises should always be slow and sustained. It's not about whipping out some crunches or even shaping the abs to be a certain way. It's about learning control of the core. Dancers can only gain that through controlled focus.

Classroom professionalism

A critical aspect of a studio environment ripe for learning is proper etiquette. Without a culture of expectations and professionalism, dance class can become more of an act of babysitting or a time filler. Even with adult students, a lack of professionalism takes away from progression. Dance class can only become a place of real learning if dancers (and parents) are expected to maintain a level of professionalism.

In Chapter 1, I talked about a class that I struggled with. The behavior of those dancers was inappropriate for class, and they did not progress well because of it. I should have come into that class with clear expectations as the baseline of behavior.

Also, one summer I observed a class by a professional guest teacher who was teaching our studio dancers at a workshop. The behavior I saw in some of the dancers that day shocked me and solidified in my mind the need for proper etiquette in dance class. Some of the students were acting disrespectful–talking, interrupting, and leaving the studio in the middle of exercises and instruction. They didn't seem malicious in their behavior, but they were too casual and just plain immature. Those dancers later received a pointed lesson from our director on what behavior is unacceptable and how we should present ourselves in class.

These kinds of experiences have solidified in me the need to set expectations for etiquette in my students.

So these are some basics of etiquette that I think dancers need to understand to take class seriously and get the most out of their time in the studio:

1. **Timeliness.** Always begin on time and end on time. We want our students to know that time in the studio is valuable. Timeliness also supports an emphasis on a proper warm-up. I tell my students that if they are late and they miss warming up at the beginning of class, they will have to sit and observe and take notes instead of dancing that day. Lay the expectation, and leave it up to your dancers (and parents) to stick to it. You can enforce this unapologetically if you are also timely–begin class on time and end on time. Your students will value class time if you set the example and value their time.

2. **Proper dance attire.** Different genres of dance will require different dress codes for class. However, lay out your expectations for apparel at the beginning and maintain them. Dressing correctly creates a feeling of uniformity and attention to detail and avoids unnecessary distractions (redoing hair and adjusting clothing causes many distractions in class). Remind your dancers they can only receive accurate feedback on their technique when they dress in a way that allows you to see their alignment and movement. There is a reason for the rule; it's not just to exert control over your students.

3. **Respect for teachers and peers.** Expect dancers to participate–not just watch during the entire class. They should experience the movement exercises with you. Don't tolerate talking on the side during instruction or exercises or belittling or talking over others. If you have laid the expectation, then you can correct it unapologetically if it happens.

4. **Use proper terms.** Use words like "tendu devant and fermé" instead of "point forward and close" to raise the level of your class. Use whatever codified terms make sense for the genre you are teaching. Also, using proper anatomical language will boost your students' maturity level and knowledge of vocabulary. It's small but impactful. Appropriate terms add to the class's focused approach, and we want our dancers to become fluent with their dance terminology. I am still personally working on this one–but I find it valuable and needed in our perpetually casual modern world.

5. **Respect for studio space.** Do not budge concerning respect to studio equipment. Do not let dancers hang on the barres like monkeys or bounce exercise balls (or bounce *on* them). My dancers know that if they are playing with the equipment, they lose their privilege to use it that day. Respecting the physical studio space/class materials is a manageable portion of etiquette to enforce because it is tangible and definable.

It is harder to begin classes with soft expectations and then try and rein in disruptive behavior later. It is much easier to start with a stricter approach toward the non-negotiables of etiquette than to try and add these things after the fact.

Some professional schools and studio environments will not tolerate anything less than these expectations, and the parents and students understand and commit to adhering to them from the outset. But not every studio environment or public school can maintain that level of control. Therefore, it is ultimately up to us as teachers to enforce what we will allow during our studio time. We can ask our students to rise to the expectations and discipline that will make their dance experience more fulfilling and productive.

Musicality

Having solid technique is one thing, but dancing musically is a nuance that creates dynamics and feeling and brings the whole performance together. Discussing musicality is one of those areas in the dance field that could fill multiple books and several courses. I was fortunate enough to take some classes regarding music for dancers in my BFA program, but not everyone has that opportunity. So, solely for brevity and simplicity, I want to share the basic ideas that have driven my teaching on the subject and helped me bring a little more musicality to my dancers.

1. **Plan ahead of time**. Create playlists or select specific music that will support your goals for particular exercises. At the very least, plan the general speed and meter for your exercises–fast or slow speed, duple (2/4, 4/4), or triple (3/4, 6/8) meters. If you are using music that is not designed for a dance class (i.e. pop songs), listen to it beforehand to make sure it carries a steady beat and doesn't change tempo or time signature.

2. **Enforce concepts with music**. Plan music that will enforce elements you are working on. If you don't know all the music forms, ask yourself what adjectives describe the music. Is it heavy, powerful, light, or bouncy? Do you need something more staccato or more sustained? Then match it up to the movement in which you want to see those qualities. Explain to the students how you want them to

perform the exercise and point out how the music mirrors that quality. A song labeled as a "tendu" doesn't necessarily have to be used for a tendu exercise. Look more for music that matches your goals for that specific combination.

3. **Imitate your music**. Try to imitate your chosen music's feeling, counts, and tempo when explaining an exercise. If you demonstrate these aspects, you can give dancers a sense of the music even before they hear the piece. Demonstrating dance combinations musically is also a crucial skill if you enjoy the privilege of having an accompanist. Then when the dancers start moving to the music, they already have some of the musicality in their bodies. Finally, make sure the piece you choose maintains the tempo you want to see in your dancers.

4. **Incorporate breath**. Emphasize deep and focused breathing and encourage fullness of movement to bring out more depth and musicality in your dancers. In Thinking Body, Dancing Mind the authors say, "[When you focus on breath] your muscles become more flexible and fluid, and your performance improves."[5] Breath relaxes tension from the body. It can bring life even to small movements and to the moments of quiet in-between steps.

I have spent an inordinate amount of time searching for just the right piece of music for choreography for performances. But do I always pick the music for practicing exercises in class with the same intentional drive? Not always. However, when I do it makes a notable difference to use music intentionally, and it saves class time. So, like the other nuances in class, we can't slap music on at the end. Instead, we need to incorporate it as we teach our dancers.

Some students are naturally musical, but we can teach anyone to dance more musically by making them more aware of how the music can drive their dancing. Music is not just running alongside dance movement like a parallel highway. Instead, music intertwines with dance like a braid with hundreds of strands winding together to one endpoint. Musicality drives dancers to express themselves and the audience to feel more deeply. Musicality can separate dance from basic exercise and drives the art form to greater depths and heights.

Pointe work

Explaining the constants of pointe work is also vast and daunting, but I want to address it briefly. Pointe work is the culmination of the main constants from Chapters 3 through 5–alignment, reaching through the extremities, and rotation. I want to address it here because pointe work is a true test of the nuances of the constants of movement, and it is somewhat of a right of passage for ballet dancers. But if we do not emphasize the right things, pointe work is a struggle and a weeding out of those dancers who might have otherwise stayed with dance.

Teaching beginner pointe has become a passion of mine over the years. And the more I reflect on my pointe training and teaching, the more I realize that we often stray too quickly from the basics that make pointe work successful. And we know that it is much more challenging to retrain than to just train well from the beginning.

The irony is that dancers have to be mature and advanced enough to begin pointe, but they should not start advanced level pointe work. Pointe work starts back at the beginning and builds up slowly, just like beginning dance training all over again. Though dancers beginning with pointe should hopefully already have the drive and maturity to work through the tedious training that pointe work requires. So, aside from discussing the ideal time/age for starting pointe training, these suggestions assume your dancers are mature and adequately trained enough to begin pointe.

Some studios and dance programs require particular pointe shoes for their students. There are several reasons directors may want to require a specific shoe, which is up to them. They might want a uniform look or prefer shoes that need more strength to work through, etc. However, I think the approach to teaching pointe work is more important than the specific shoes that the dancers wear, so I won't address the nuances of pointe shoe fitting here. The essence is the same, no matter what shoe your dancers wear. These concepts are under the assumption that dancers are wearing well-fitted shoes.

We don't want to take dancers who are on the right track, put them in pointe shoes, and then continue from where we left off in their technique shoes after a few lessons on how to break in a pointe shoe. Pointe work is more than just learning to mold shoes to work with the feet. Instead, it is more conditioning and molding of the foot to control the added complication of a pointe shoe. Pointe work has to be taken slow, and not just for a month or two. Pointe work requires a focus on the basics for the long haul. I often keep my dancers doing fundamental strengthening and slow movement for the first year, only occasionally adding new challenges.

To a dancer just starting pointe, it often feels like waiting for a pot to boil. They just want the pot to boil and wonder why it's taking so long! They have waited and worked, and they feel like they have arrived when they finally get the go-ahead to train in pointe shoes.

But it will take time for their skills to "come to a boil" as they retrain their beginner skills in pointe shoes.

But students who learn to approach their pointe work the correct way will not feel tortured by small increments of progress. Instead, they will recognize the bigger picture. It takes mental fortitude to wait for the water to warm up to a boil in slow increments without wondering if time has stalled. But those students who can see the bigger picture will learn to prepare other parts of their training and realize that those parts contribute to their whole training.

It's challenging for a dancer to envision the bigger picture and have the patience to get there. So, it is common for dancers to feel like pointe work moves slowly–if they are training correctly. Again, the basics can't be skipped over, but you should teach them unapologetically. Bringing water to a rolling boil cannot be sped up–it simply takes time.

My approach to pointe work is sticking to a few basics and insisting that my dancers learn them before they expand their pointe experience. There isn't any pomp and frill when beginning pointe work. All of the following ideas are a significant focus of my pointe classes, and they all hearken back to the same principles–simplicity and precision.

Coming down from pointe:

I often tell my dancers that going up on pointe is the easier thing to do (though no pointe work is actually "easy"). Coming down requires immense amounts of control and strength. Dancers descending from pointe should always begin with a lift and stay lifted as they come down to flat feet. This forces dancers to roll through their entire shoe instead of plopping down from full pointe to demi-pointe with a noticeable drop.

There are a few ways to get this idea across, but insisting on consistency with coming down with control is the crucial thing.

- Sometimes I have my dancers think of reaching down from a high stool or other high ledge and stretching their toes down to reach the floor. The imagery helps to think of lengthening and lifting before coming down from pointe.

- Other times we imagine a double elevator–one elevator is going up under the heel, and one is going down slowly through the ball of the foot. The imagery of opposing forces provides more control for the descent.

- I also ask dancers to simply attempt to lift higher in their shoes and feel their toes attempt to spread apart as they come down. The effort it takes to focus on spreading out each toe forces them to slow down and control their descent.

- One way to build strength in the metatarsals for coming down is to perform toe "push-ups" and just practice going from demi to full pointe for several repetitions–always avoiding plunking or snapping in or out of demi-pointe.

Slow tempos are vital in all of these practices.

Rolling through the feet:

Learning to use every part of the foot is essential for building strength and control. The only way to train this is to do it every class. Practice in parallel. Practice in first position. Roll through the feet to full pointe and back down with straight legs. Practice again with plie. Do it slowly in each class and watch for sustained movement without emphasizing one single part. If there is any popping or accents in the movement (often through the demi-pointe), slow it down or do it again. This is the perfect time to focus on alignment and rotation as well since those will support the feet from above.

Using two feet:

It is tempting to take a dancer at their current level, fit them in pointe shoes, and expect to continue where they left off. However, continuing at the same level is detrimental to the core basics of technique. Dancers have to relearn those core basics in their pointe shoes. Even a basic tendu becomes a new challenge in pointe shoes because weight placement has to shift more than before and the metatarsals have to work harder to point the foot.

Dancers can build strength and confidence for pointe in simpler movements. So, instead of letting dancers continue their training with movements from one foot like soutenus, piqués, relevés in cou-de-pied or retiré, pas de bourrées, etc., focus on movements only from two feet starting out. Use more exercises like relevés, échappés, simple sautés from two feet and landing on two feet, bourrées, preparations for chaînés and (eventually) turning chaînés, etc. It just requires a diligent and persistent teacher to make sure all of those movements are executed precisely. This is where our mantra, "teach the basics and don't apologize for them," is vital because dancers want to hurry through this part of their training more than ever before.

We should not complicate pointe-specific classes—they are a training ground. They are an opportunity to slow down and refine the technique once again. And through all of the training, proper alignment, rotation, and reaching must be present and constant. If your dancers begin to struggle with one or more of the main constants, take another step back.

If their pelvis has an anterior/posterior tilt, pointe work will magnify it, and your dancers will lose their lift and connection to their abdominals. If their rotational strength is lacking, pointe will magnify it, and your students will lose their stability to control the direction of their legs. If your dancers' feet are not fully lifted and extended, it will be magnified in their pointe shoes and will cause knuckling and unstable ankles. All of these things can be injurious if we are not careful. However, the time and focus put into pointe will be rewarding when we do not skim through it.

<u>Summary of Chapter Six</u>

- The nuances of dance training extend beyond learning how to move correctly.

- Among these nuances of dance training are proper warm-up, etiquette, musicality, and pointe work.

- The teacher's commitment to these disciplines will set the tone for the class and create a professional work environment where students can progress.

7

Simplify

Have a vision. Have a theme. Have a plan.

IN RECENT YEARS THERE has been a movement toward minimalism and living more simply. I see it in the trending popularity of tiny homes and books/shows about organizing and tidying up–people like Marie Kondo[6] have become common household names. Simplifying clears up physical and mental space leaving only what is essential and valuable.

You can also simplify your time in the studio and how you teach dance technique.

As a dance instructor, you are tasked with teaching positions, alignment, rotation, balance, musicality, coordination, spatial awareness, flexibility, pointed feet, reaching through the space, choreography, and the list goes on. Learning to dance can be a lifetime pursuit with all there is to know. So simplifying is not just a nice idea, but it is a necessity in training dancers.

If you place equal importance on everything, nothing seems important. When something is unique or essential to your class, it needs to stand out. It can be challenging for your dancers to know what to focus on and what holds the most weight. They rely on you for direction and guidance to focus their thoughts and efforts.

Imagine you are in a session with a personal trainer. Your trainer starts by giving you slow abdominal sit-ups to work your deep core muscles. He tells you that strong abdominals are crucial to your training. So you focus intently on your abdominals as you begin to roll up and down through the sit-up slowly.

Then before you could barely get through more than a rep or two, your trainer urgently shoves weights into your hands and says that your biceps are also very important for lifting things. You agree. Bicep strength is necessary too, so you add it in.

As you focus on both your sit-ups and your bicep curls, your trainer adds ankle weights and says you should be additionally extending your legs and getting those quadriceps to fire. So you add that in as you continue your slow and focused sit-ups and bicep curls.

Your trainer then reminds you to keep deep breaths flowing. In and out. Focus on relaxing and breathing deeply through each movement.

You do your best to juggle all of it, but you lose your attention to detail with the mental and physical gymnastics. After your session, you aren't sure if you feel accomplished or defeated.

This whole scenario is a little ridiculous and counterproductive. Your imaginary trainer is overwhelming you, and you are not benefiting much from it.

It's hyperbolic, but it simply illustrates an important concept: we can only focus on so much at once. We all have physical and mental limitations. And while multi-tasking seems possible, learning something that we want to retain will require focus. Sometimes that means narrowing our focus until we increase our tolerance and ability.

Sometimes we unintentionally put our students through similar stress and confusion. All the while, they try to keep up and do their best. Everything we ask them to do *is* essential to their training. But they are burdened with the dilemma of deciding what to focus on and what to let go of this time. They might choose a different focus than we had envisioned.

The adage comes to mind that a person can be a "jack of all trades, and a master of none." Likewise, the sheer number of things you ask your students to do does not equate to the quality. Although dancers are known for being decent multi-taskers, we need to narrow our focus for our students to better set them up for success.

As the teacher, you drive the whole class with a focus. Instead of saying everything that comes to mind that you learned in your training, choose one or two things to hone into. Then everyone can progress in the same direction.

Some dancers may have specific needs. You can address those independently but have a guiding direction you want to see the class members work toward as a whole.

Do you want them to perform all of their technique exercises correctly? Of course. Should you ask them to do *all* of it right now? Not necessarily. Ask yourself what you want your students to understand today.

Work concept by concept. Step by step. Have a focus and simplify.

Simplifying is challenging. As a teacher, I am looking at the whole picture. I can see what is not working, where my students have gaps in understanding, and what I want them to understand. However, I am not doing my students any favors to nitpick everything on every exercise all in one day.

That doesn't mean we can't challenge our students. On the contrary, it is helpful to learn to juggle more than one thing as a dancer. Eventually, you want your students to work out what they need to focus on for themselves. However, your expectations can evolve and open up by degrees over time. I call it "the funnel approach" to lesson planning.

Picture the shape of a funnel. One end is long and narrow and can only allow small or single objects to pass through to the wider end. And the wider end can collect multiple objects that feed into the narrow end.

One way to simplify your plan for your students is to picture this funnel image. Information for your students should begin narrowly and at a slower rate. It comes in smaller doses, just like the small end of the funnel. Then, as your dancers can more fully grasp those smaller doses of concepts, they can start to open up to additional concepts. They can begin to collect more information at a time just as the wider end of the funnel opens up.

The funnel image also applies in reverse. If your students are more advanced, you can give them several things to focus on in succession. You can provide them with a list of concepts you want to see from them. But reverse your funnel image to where the wide end now feeds into the smaller end. A lot of information or a list of expectations should still lead to a narrower focus.

At the end of this chapter, there is an example of how to plan your classes with this funnel approach.

Teaching steps with simplicity

Simplifying and choosing a focus is not settling for less, just like focusing on the basics. It actually allows for *more* of a particular thing that you are focusing on. It is deep diving and no longer snorkeling on the surface. Expand and add to a concept, then circle back and revisit. Repeat and repeat.

I want my students to catch onto my larger vision for class. So, when I begin my classes, I briefly explain my plan for the day and the goals I have for my dancers. Telling my students my general plan and goals for them that day holds me to it. And it helps my dancers know what they can put their efforts toward during that particular class.

There are different ways I approach planning my class with a specific focus or theme in mind:

One way I focus in class is by working on **several aspects of one specific step** throughout the class. Gretchen Ward Warren also recommends this logic in her book *Classical Ballet Technique*. She says, "I find it best to begin the preparations for my classes from the [final, most difficult jump to be studied that day] and work backwards. [...] The more often a movement coordination is repeated in all its various forms within the same class, the better the student will learn it."[7]

For example, if we need to work on assemblé, all of our exercises will be centered around the pieces that make up assemblé. So, first, we would work on brushing the floor in plié tendu. Then we may work on going from an extended leg to a sous-sus. Next, we might work on the accent and timing of sous-sus in spring relévés and practice coordinating the port de bras, and we could also work on sautés from a single leg.

When I create a focused lesson plan like this, I take all of my exercises and look at them through the lens of the specific step we are working on.

Another way I can simplify my class is to **focus on a specific concept**. For example, one time in class, I wanted to condition my dancers to fully use the space around them. I gave them one word: "width." We explored how rotation and deep pliés help the legs open wide. We talked about how opening the shoulders and reaching the arms long in the second position creates width in the upper body. We practiced having a broad focus with our eyes and looking beyond our personal space. We focused everything on that one word: "width."

It turned out to be a good class. It brought a fresh perspective to exercises that were otherwise precisely the same as the last time we met together.

You could also **name a focus or goal for each specific exercise** rather than one focus for the entire class. For example, your focus can be alignment for pliés, weight placement for tendus, reaching in rond de jambes, etc.

However, I would caution again that too many directions to focus on will weaken the lesson learned.

If you take a rope and pull apart all of the strands, each strand is much weaker on its own. Each strand contributes to the whole, but they are not as durable alone. Likewise, it is best to tie everything together with a central purpose or theme if you have a lot to work on with your students (which is always the case with dance class). If there is something glaringly incorrect or something that will cause injury, address it. Otherwise, just stick to your focus.

Teaching with a focused approach

Here are some more specific ways that I help my students focus and learn more efficiently:

1. Talk less, dance more

If you use too many words, most will be lost. Try not to lecture, and keep things concise.

Any of my previous students would laugh ironically at this advice. I am hardly at a loss for something to say about how or what they should be working on. Because of that, though, I know the downfall as a teacher if you talk too much.

If something you are working on requires a lot of discussion and exploration, make sure your dancers are not just standing by and watching you. Instead, involve them in the discovery. Ask them to experiment and feel it for themselves. Again, this idea goes back to the etiquette of class. We should expect our dancers to participate–not just sit and wait. Dancers will not improve if they do not try things out in their own bodies.

We will discuss more benefits of "talking less and dancing more" in Chapter 12, but the critical thing to remember is that sometimes less is more. Simplicity goes a long way.

2. Creativity loves constraint

Now, don't solidify the foundations in your dancers and then turn around and throw it out the window when it comes to choreography. This is another thing I learned from wise directors and mentors around me, and I have found it to be invaluable: *Only give your dancers steps to perform in their choreography that they have mastered.*

In the book *The Intimate Act of Choreography*, the authors state the idea that, "A dance should have no unnecessary parts; this requires not that the choreographer make all his dances short nor that he avoid all detail, but that every moment tell."[8] We want our students to be able to fully "tell" the steps they have mastered for performance.

Performance time for students is not the time to whip out tricks and experimental movements. Instead, choreographing is the perfect time to simplify. It can be tricky to fight the urge to create a show-stopping piece of choreography packed with all of your favorite ideas. It takes humility and honesty with yourself to decide what ideas to keep and what to save for another day.

When it comes time to choreograph for my students, I make a list of steps they execute well. I allow myself to include steps they are on track to mastering when their performance comes around (knowing that I may have to adapt or simplify later if needed). I have even taken combinations we have done in class and spliced them together with their role/character in mind. One year I even took an entire petit allegro exercise we had been working on and put it directly in a part of choreography that made sense for the performance. We just layered it with different dancers doing it in different directions simultaneously and added some entrances and exits. The dancers had already been practicing it, and they performed confidently.

Here are some visual examples of this concept of carrying technique exercises over onto the stage:

(**Above**) We worked on basic technique exercises in different body directions in class and used that concept directly as an element of our choreography.

(**Above**) We worked heavily on retiré passé and used that skill in our choreography. The only thing we changed for the stage was the arm positions.

Some of these ideas may sound limiting or basic, but if I have learned anything about choreography, it's that rules help you become more creative and develop motifs in your movement. If anything, choreography, for young students especially, will become much less stressful this way.

This can even work for students who you are not as familiar with. For example, one year, I had an experience coming as a guest and setting some choreography for a local high school dance company. The dancers had a wide range of abilities, and I had limited rehearsal time. To make anything work, I just had to keep my movement motifs uncomplicated. They could evolve a bit, but the base of all of the movement was simple and repeatable. It turned out to be a nice piece overall, and I was able to utilize all of the dancers' abilities. It was a lesson for me that our movement does not have to be complicated or full of tricks to create enjoyable choreography.

I have taken dance improvisation classes, and most of what we did in those classes was create rules to develop movement phrases. We would rarely just dance improvisationally without a set of regulations or restrictions. And the result was often beautiful movement phrases. Choreographic rules simplify and create a focus from your broad library of movement vocabulary. So, instead of giving yourself free rein of all the steps you know, give yourself free rein of the steps your students know.

If your students have a limited movement vocabulary of steps they have mastered (especially beginners, new dancers on pointe, or young students), then explore what you can do with those few steps. Use different timing. Change the port de bras. Layer, overlap, and create cannons of the same movement. Change formation and body directions. For advanced dancers, you can even reverse steps they have been working on to create more exciting and intricate movements. All of this can be done without sacrificing the integrity and quality of the steps your dancers know.

Simplification also does not mean it will be uninteresting. But as a reflection on you, you want your students to show well. So rather than having complicated movements, focus on the intricate details and nuances of simple exercises. Well-executed slow and simple movements are much more impressive than a sloppy mess of partially and poorly executed steps.

The common phrase "creativity loves constraint" also applies to daily technique exercises. A few shorter exercises are often more effective than fitting the same amount into just one movement combination. Give your dancers brief exercises with a direct and central focus.

3. Learn to let go

Learning to let go of good ideas is another way to simplify choreography and class exercises. Letting go is a vital skill in keeping focus and simplifying. Scrap what is not working or whatever isn't highlighting your students' strengths. I address this more in Chapter 10, but it is a large part of simplifying and worth mentioning here as well.

Letting go could mean reworking part (or all) of a combination if your students struggle to understand a concept. It could mean taking a single pirouette down to a strong balance instead. It could mean slowing down the timing of something instead of doing it at your original intended speed.

Letting go could mean many things. I often ask myself these questions about class exercises and choreography to decide what I need to rework:

- Does the movement work for my students' needs and the curriculum they should be learning?

- Does this choreography showcase their best work?

- What lessons am I teaching them when I insist on keeping my original plan even when it is not working?

- What lessons am I teaching them when I am willing to let things go to find a better way?

These questions are on a continuous loop in my brain as a teacher.

Several years ago, I had a perfect crash course in simplifying quickly and learning to scrap what wasn't working.

I was a finalist in a choreography competition with a local professional ballet company. The dancers were all accomplished and talented. Coming from mainly teaching amateur dancers in local studios, I felt somewhat out of my league working with them. But I had many ideas and wanted to see them work out.

The tricky part was that we had a limited time constraint. We had about 9 hours of rehearsal to set and clean an 8-10 minute original work.

The dancers were competent professionals, but even they could not make all of my ideas come to life as I envisioned in that amount of time. We couldn't workshop and develop each idea. It was no fault of theirs. I just had to make a judgment call, or I would be stuck with an incomplete piece of choreography.

Ultimately, I wanted my choreography to look polished. So I had to scrap what wasn't working and adapt quickly to focus on what would work. I had to simplify my process. There was no time to overthink or over analyze. First, I had to decide what would showcase well and help guide my intentions with my piece. Then, if the movement didn't fit those criteria, I had to let go and save it for another project.

The piece came together, and I was satisfied and happy with how it turned out. Simplifying helped my process because it forced me not to waste too much time or energy.

On the flip side, I have had teachers who scrap what they are doing choreographically *every* class–that's not what I am saying to do.

There was a particular time I was a young dancer when we were learning choreography for a performance, and the choreographer started over at every rehearsal. The movement, music, spacing–everything was different each rehearsal. It was more than just tweaking things that weren't working–it was lacking any sort of guiding focus. If my memory serves me well, that particular piece of choreography was never even finished or performed.

That's not simplification. It is a poor use of time.

In a performance, the audience doesn't know what they are missing or what might have been. The audience wouldn't be sad if that double pirouette was initially supposed to be a triple–especially if it is done well. So don't be afraid to say something is not working, and don't be scared to take a step back to something more basic. Students must understand the value of quality over quantity.

4. Unapologetic repetition

We live in a culture that defies repetition and monotony. We want new and exciting all the time, and we often get it with so many advances in technology. But there is great value in learning to repeat things and be okay with that use of time.

Practice is when you correctly repeat something to learn it. Part of simplifying is not being afraid of that correct repetition. Remember my ballet director who asked us to teach the same exercises all year to the same group of young beginners? At first, I thought that was a wild request, but I saw beautiful things when I took her advice. It stretched me as a teacher. It pushed my dancers.

Repeat exercises that are short and simple. Use the repetition to watch for all of the finer details and nuances you expect in that exercise (like hand shape, foot shape, head directions, etc.).

Repeat exercises that your students are struggling to grasp fully. Make the adaptations or corrections needed, and then repeat them.

Repeat movements in choreography. Choreography can be simplified with repetition of the same movement. It can be layered with different facing, timing, or speeds to add more excitement or interest. But the movement can still be repeated.

Repeat. Repeat. Repeat. Your dancers will learn the value of continuing to try and work to gain a skill. Repeating exercises to ingrain a skill teaches perseverance.

Final thoughts on simplifying your teaching

There are many benefits to simplifying your class with a focus:

1. Simplifying and keeping a driving focus gives your students grace. They have more chances to get it right and learn it more permanently. For example: if they can't quite grasp the idea of how to move their weight to their standing leg, remind them they have many chances *today* to work on it. They will get to work on weight transfers in every exercise.

2. Simplifying class with a central focus allows you to be more patient with your dancers. You know that they will get it because you will give them multiple chances to practice it and get it right.

3. You will get better results from your students. They will feel more confident in attacking a correction head-on if they know what to focus on and what exactly it will help. Repetition in different applications will drive it home if your entire class exercises are geared to the same one or two concepts.

Example of a funnel approach while lesson planning:

Teaching with a funnel approach is like layering concepts little by little and continuing to circle back to the foundation. It's not a complicated idea, but it is a skill to be able to take complicated steps and break them down into simpler parts to be put back together again. Take one main focus and slowly add new concepts a little at a time without letting your dancers leave the original focus behind.

Here is an example of how I might layer concepts starting with younger/beginning students (who begin learning at the narrow base of the funnel)–taking into account that this concept of progressing wider along the "funnel" can take months, even years, for some understanding to take shape. Dancers will learn through your persistence that it is a long process that takes time:

1. Have a sole focus on teaching alignment (the first constant), and find it in each of the positions. Find alignment in basic movements–pliés, tendus, and so on. Find alignment while practicing port de bras. Any exercise you teach, you can focus on achieving basic skeletal alignment. Even as you add more movements throughout the class, proper alignment is still the goal and central focus.

2. Once alignment is coming more naturally to your students (not necessarily within the same class but over time), then add another focus. Your next focus could be constants two and three–reaching through the extremities and rotation–or something else you think is necessary. Layer these ideas on *top* of your expectations with alignment, not

instead of focusing on alignment. Keep revisiting alignment as you add a new focus. If your dancers can begin to regularly apply all of these concepts, then you can layer once again.

3. As you progress to more complicated steps like accented dégagés, rond de jambe en l'air, développé, grand jetés, etc., then tie those back to the same basics you began with. More complicated steps incorporate more than one basic factor. For example: Rond de jambe tests alignment while reaching and rotating. Grand jeté builds on grand battement, which comes from dégagé, which is built on tendu, which comes from reaching and engaging rotation. Any larger or more complicated step should be tied to the basic understanding beneath it. Outline to your students the concept of connecting to the basics even in the more complicated movements.

4. Then continue onto multi-factored movements that compound the basic steps your dancers have been learning. You can explain that something like a pas de basque combines several concepts like rond de jambe, jeté, cou-de-pied, and (sometimes glissé) to tendu. Then break it down further for your students and remind them of the concepts that build each of those. Layering concepts wider out in the funnel should always stay tied to what is at the base.

As students become more advanced, their movement vocabulary is more vast and requires a lot of different focuses. Just be sure to continually tie things back to the building blocks that make all of those complicated steps possible. Let the funnel grow out and compound as they advance, then let it all circle back into the central focal point of the basics.

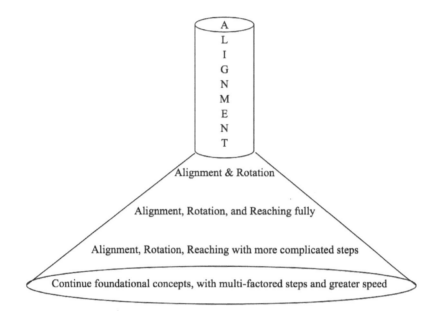

Summary of Chapter Seven

- Simplifying our teaching reduces the stress placed on our students and gives them the ability to focus on what we want them to.

- A funnel approach to lesson planning allows us to focus on the basics and compound what our students are learning when they are ready.

- Some ways you can simplify your teaching are lecturing less, limiting and making rules for ourselves in choreography, and repeating concepts for our students.

8

Engage

Teach "why" and "how"

ONE YEAR FOR SPRING break, instead of going on a mini-vacation as a family, we opted to spend some of our vacation money on board games and card games to play together. We stocked up on games we had been eyeing for a while. We also took a chance on some games we had never played or heard of before.

The games that were geared toward young children were easy to pick up and play. The rules were simple and the games didn't require too much focus or thought.

When we got to some of the more advanced games, I struggled to pick up on some of the rules. It was challenging to keep track of the nuances and exceptions–let alone learn some strategy.

One particular game took almost an hour to read through the instructions and figure out how the game was played. I couldn't use any strategy to win the game at first because I was mostly just trying to remember the rules. And because no one in our family had played before, we were all floundering a bit.

It might have been easier to learn the game with a more experienced player leading the way. An experienced player could have engaged us in the gameplay and helped us understand the rules and the strategy. It would have been helpful instead of us only reading the rule book. Having someone talk through the rules would have made the learning process easier and probably more enjoyable.

Similarly, learning dance technique is like learning an advanced board game. There are a myriad of "rules" and checklists to keep in mind. And without your more experienced help to engage their brains, your dancers will go through the motions, and it may take longer for them to understand how to "win" the game. It will take longer for them to learn to be autonomous "players" who are authentic and strategic in their dancing. However, engaging our dancers gets them to problem solve, become invested, and explore the exercises independently.

Dancer engagement is crucial to crossing the threshold from rule copying to invested and independent dancing. We don't want to teach dancers to be copy-ers. We want to train dancers to be artists. That begins with engaging and investing them in the work they are doing. We want our dancers to move from reciting the rules to dancing strategically to "win."

It's similar to when you learn to drive a car. Sitting and reading the car manual about the buttons and gears is one thing. It's another to sit in the driver's seat and experience it.

Sometimes I watch my students and sense a general feeling of blandness in their dancing. Their movement is rote and disconnected. When that happens, the phrase "dead on arrival" comes to mind and I remind them not to mosey through the steps.

That feeling of monotony is bound to happen with how much repetition dance training requires. But when I see my students reach that point of bland dancing, I know I need to create more momentum, refresh my students' perspective, and engage them in their movement once again. We don't want them to approach class leisurely.

If your students know the "why" behind the rules, they can engage in the movement in an authentic way.

In my mind, engagement is synonymous with investment. If you are engaging your students, they become uniquely invested. They begin to care and want to succeed on their own when it starts making sense to them personally. If your dancers have something to relate to, they can gain more from your class.

I have had teachers (and I have been the teacher) who forgets the larger vision. Is the idea to turn out technicians? Is our goal as teachers to create copies of what we deem a successful dancer to be? Or is our broader vision to develop self-regulating individual thinkers?

Keep your dancers' minds engaged with different ways of looking at technique and envisioning steps–then their learning will be more efficient and long-lasting. Then they will achieve that broader vision we want for them. Engagement happens on a personal and internal level, so to reach each student, we would do well to teach in a variety of ways.

The saying "all work and no play makes Jack a dull boy" is true. Dance is not meant to be dull or work for work's sake. What are we doing if it's not enjoyable? Engagement makes dance more fun and fulfilling.

Young dancers, in particular, can't always make a connection and understand a concept if you simply tell them verbally to point their toes. They can't always isolate their abdominal muscles or rotators without a visual or targeted exercise to help get those muscles to fire. It reminds me of the well-known Confucian saying: "Tell me, and I'll forget. Show me, and I may remember. Involve me, and I learn." Dance education is not for spectators. It requires engaged repetition and involvement for long-lasting learning to happen.

The following ideas are things I consider when trying to engage my students in class. I will explain each idea in the correlating sections:

1. Teach progressions, 2. Teach in contrast, 3. Use props, 4. Incorporate reward systems, 5. Ask questions, 6. Use imagery, 7. Incorporate literature, 8. Use easy sayings and quick cues. You can even show your dancers pictures and videos (of themselves or others) of what you are trying to convey.

Use these ideas as a starting point to form your own engaging lessons. The key is to use many methods to successfully teach the variety of students you will encounter.

8 Tips for Engaging Students

1. Address the "why" and "how" through progression

Children are notorious for repeatedly asking "why" and "how" things are, and as adults, we want to know the same things. It is our nature to want to understand something for ourselves and not just do it because we are told.

Answering why or how something is done gives context and purpose to what we are doing. And understanding the physics and practicality of a step (not just the aesthetic, since that looks different for everyone) is essential in understanding why we even bother with specific steps in dance.

Dancers will become engaged if we can answer their questions of "why" and "how." If we can answer either of those questions, our students will care more to see it through. They will understand the benefit of what we are asking them to do. We are not just asking them to repeat their dégagés to torture them—we want to build up their abilities for what lies ahead.

Teaching the progression of steps helps to build a broader vision in dancers. It gives them a view of how a particular dance step is essential in the bigger picture.

I often tell my students that I care more about them understanding why we do things than I do about them copying their peers or me. Dancing is not for cookie cutters. The best dancing does not come from a mold.

Older students can more easily see the correlation between cause and effect, but younger students can also develop this skill if you bring it to their attention. With practice, dancers can become great problem solvers. They will see *why* they are working on tendus. They will understand that it is for a greater purpose than just pointing their foot in a specific direction. If they know that a tendu progresses into the skills for extensions and jumps, they can see the purpose in a plain old tendu.

I often remind my students where mastering a specific step or skill can lead them. It helps them envision what they need to do or what is holding them back. Then, when they become proficient at something, they can advance along with the progression. Here are some examples of progressions you can easily outline to your students:

Flat feet progressing to relevé or pointe:

Standing on flat feet, without rolling in the arches → Balance on one foot, arch lifted and rotation engaged. Possibly coupled with other movements á terre (on the floor) → Relevé/demi-pointe on two feet → Relevé/demi-pointe on one foot. Possibly connected with other actions en l'air (off the floor) → Jumps/pointe work from two feet and then one. (This progression is demonstrated **below**)

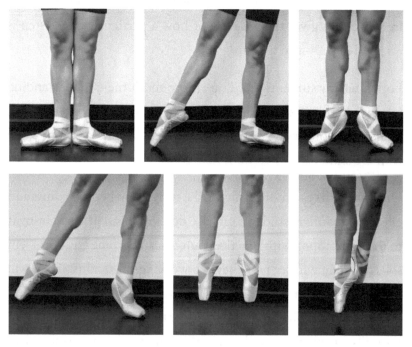

This example is not necessarily a progression of steps, but a progression of concepts. At each progression, dancers learn an additional skill that will lead to the next difficulty level.

Dancers have to understand the first before they can grasp the second version of the progression, and so on. If dancers do not understand the original concept of weight equally distributed throughout two balanced feet flat on the floor, everything beyond that will be much more challenging to execute.

Tendu progressing to larger steps:

Tendu (brushing on the floor) → dégagé (brushing barely off the floor) → glissades (small jump with a similar brushing concept). Or a similar progression: Tendu (brushing the floor) → Grand battements (brushing largely off the floor) → Grand jeté (large jump with the same brushing concept). (This progression is demonstrated **below**.)

Arguably, tendu is the beginning to many progressions in dance. These are just a couple. The idea is to explain the connection of those steps to your dancers.

Cou-de-pied progressing to full extensions:

Cou-de-pied position → cou-de-pied progressing up to retiré → cou-de-pied, progressing through retiré, then to full développé/extensions.

You can lay out the progression of *any* step. These are just basic examples.

It's straightforward if you just look at the steps listed out in sequence like that. In fact, it is an oversimplification. But explaining the progression gives a road map of where basic steps can lead. I want my students to see the connections just as simply. If my dancers are having difficulty seeing the purpose of an exercise, I want them to see the next level we are trying to get to.

How can you show your students what they are progressing toward?

Let's look at the first progression of steps I outlined. I can explain to my students that standing flat-footed is just the first step. The next step is to be able to rise to relevé. That is when I can show my dancers what may be holding them back from progressing to their relevé.

I can explain that they cannot move from a flat-footed position to relevé if their weight is in their heels or their arches are rolling in. They can test this quickly by letting go of support from the barre and seeing which direction their body tends to drift. If they find themselves falling backward, their misalignment is most likely in their abdominals, hips, and ribs—which we discussed in Chapter 3.

Then I can explain what they need to understand to progress to the next level.

Then I remind them that after relevé, the next goal is to rise en pointe. If dancers are sinking their heel in their relevé or pulling back in their hips, they will not be able to rise even further over a pointe shoe. It helps them see the progression they will miss out on if they continue to sit back in their heels.

Finally, teaching the progression of steps will not only aid your dancers in their dancing. If they can understand the process of how their movements fit together and build on each other, they can more naturally help future students of their own.

2. Teach by contrast

If you remember my example of the chicken dance exercise (addressed in Chapter 3), you already know I am a proponent of teaching with contrast. Contrasting what you don't want directly with what you *do* want is another way to create engagement.

Show your dancers how it doesn't work, let them try it, then show them how it should work. Contrast also adds a little bit of play in class because the dancers like a chance to stand or move in a silly way.

Take lifting the leg to the side, for example. If a dancer lifts their hip when they lift their leg, I point it out to them. I then ask them to tilt their hips and exaggerate that crooked position. Even if I try to assist them in lifting their leg with my hands, it will only go so far with a crooked hip. But then I ask them to contrast their raised hip with a dropped and level hip. As soon as they drop their hip, their leg has a pathway to rise higher, and I can lift it there to show them that pathway that is now freely open.

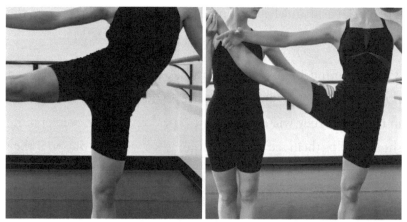

Exaggerated crooked hip vs. corrected level hip

Now it is up to the student to gain the proper strength to do that autonomously (**first image below**). And finally, with properly aligned hips their leg can swing freely and with a wider range of motion in steps like a grand battement (**second image below**).

The contrast of the lifted hip and the aligned hip gives an immediate illustration and sensation of correct versus incorrect technique.

A side benefit: contrast can also help to increase muscular flexibility. For example, if dancers resist a stretch while in the position and then release, their muscles will have further release and they will find improved flexibility.

3. Teach with props

Props can teach memorable lessons as well. They can put a name and a face to a concept or draw students in to engage with a particular idea. Collect props that are useful for many applications. I have many in my dance bag and others available at the studio where I teach. Most of them don't take up much space. Here are a few and what I use them for:

Accordion:

I address many applications for this in Chapter 3–Alignment.

Pull-back/wind up toy cars:

These take up hardly any space, and they are an excellent way to illustrate potential energy. For instance, if I want my students to understand the power in their plié, I get out the pull-back cars. First, they can see how the pull-back propels the vehicle forward. Then they can apply that concept to using their pliés down to drive their jumps vertically. It's a fun new way to frame a common concept.

Poppers:

Another good prop that I keep in my teaching bag is a large toy popper. I use it to show the power in plié coupled with rotation. Both sides have to be stretched and pried open to invert the popper and let it spring back open. It is an excellent way to illustrate the rotation and resistance needed in a preparatory plié and how that energy translates into a more powerful jump.

Parachute:

This tool is excellent for young/beginning dancers and breaks up the ordinarily strict dance class structure. A parachute helps dancers learn to move in unison and to be spatially aware. Lift the parachute and bring it down together, or chassé or bourrée in a circle as a group. It is also great for quizzing beginning dancers. Parachute down and call out a position or step. Then lift the parachute, and they should be in position. It requires quick thinking on the dancers' part to keep up with the rise and fall of the parachute. A parachute has a lot of uses and applications in a dance class.

Jumbo dice:

Something as simple as rolling dice can add engagement to otherwise regular and repetitive exercises–and it doesn't take any extra time away from class. Take an exercise your students know well and use the die to add some chance. Change the timing or number of repetitions with a roll of the dice. For example, you could use odd numbers to do it slowly and even numbers to do it more quickly. Or maybe the number they roll is how many times they repeat the exercise. Or perhaps if they roll an odd number, you begin on the left side, and for even numbers, you start on the right. The options with dice are countless (wink wink), and from my experience, dancers of all ages enjoy using it.

I have made my own large dice out of square boxes or foam squares, but buying one is very inexpensive. I also have additional dice to add some variety to the class–a colorful die, and a die with different images of body parts on it. I have used each of those in several ways over the years for dance improvisation and switching up our normal class routine.

Spatula or small shovel:

This prop is helpful when explaining tendus in conjunction with turnout. Even if your dancers can utilize their turnout in their preparatory positions, it is easy to lose as soon as they move. I remind my students that a spatula lays flat and wide for scooping, and turning a spatula or shovel on its side makes it cut through instead of scooping from underneath. Similarly, remind them to keep their foot in contact with the floor. Then their rotation then needs to work as long as possible to keep the foot flat and wide rather than letting their toes cut through the space–leaving the heel behind.

You can even use this idea in conjunction with the season to make it more memorable in their minds: In the wintertime, remind them of a snow shovel laying wide and flat and scooping underneath. In the springtime, remind them of digging up sand at the beach with a shovel. You can remind them how to scoop underneath a pancake or egg in a pan. These images can vary, but all have the same effect. It will help them envision keeping their feet spread wide and open on the floor rather than closed off and turned in. It often works!

Rock climbing harness:

I have brought a harness to class before to help dancers visualize and feel a lift from their hips to help them rise and jump more easily. It was beneficial for dancers to learn to descend from pointe as well.

Small bean bags:

I have used bean bags as hand weights in class to help dancers use their upper body with more intention and power. For example, suppose my dancers are flipping their arms out of sync with their movement and cutting through the space (which happens often in petít allégro movements). In that case, I ask them to hold bean bags in their hands and use the momentum of the weight swinging to give them more driving and full upper body movement.

Therabands and exercise balls:

Therabands (or resistance bands) can create physical feedback in an exercise or be used to strengthen specific muscle groups. Resistance bands help strengthen feet and ankles. Some programs teach ways to use therabands to wrap around the back, arms, or legs to help dancers feel certain muscle sensations. Exercise balls can be used for cross training and applying technique concepts in a different way. An excellent program that uses therabands, exercise balls and other props for conditioning and training dancers is *Progressing Ballet Technique* (PBT), developed for dancers and founded by Marie Walton-Mahon.[9]

My students doing PBT exercises in class

Dry erase marker:

This tool is another small thing I keep in my teaching bag, and I use it almost every class. It's useful for writing terms, formations, movement patterns, or quick diagrams of what we are learning on the studio mirror. Sometimes it helps dancers to see something drawn or written out. Just be sure when class is over to wipe it off the mirror thoroughly with a soft cloth or cleaner.

Stickers:

Put stickers on the parts of the body you want your students to have a visual reminder. For example: If you are talking about rotation, you can have some on the hips, knees, and feet–reminding your dancers of the critical checkpoints to think about for rotation. You can put one on their finger to help them follow their port de bras with their gaze. You can put a sticker on the tip of the nose to help dancers with spotting for turns. Stickers are inexpensive props that you can use in countless ways.

4. Use rewards

A reward system can help incentivize dancers to reach specific milestones. Rewards can help dancers feel accomplished and validated. They can also create benchmarks for your dancers to work toward.

It is possible to get too wound up and forget to have fun. Let your class have something to work toward as each dancer also works on their individual goals.

Again, we are not trying to create a militant atmosphere where only the toughest and most talented survive. Let your dancers have joy in the journey. Too often, I have taught students who are burnt out and lose their drive by the time they get to their teen years. There are many contributing factors to this, but one is simply expecting so much and not giving much in return. We know the life lessons and intrinsic value of dance training, but we may still have dancers who haven't learned those lessons quite yet. A rare extrinsic reward can refocus a dancer who might otherwise feel burnt out. It is not the only solution for burnout, but one thing to consider.

Rewards can come in several forms and don't always have to be physical items. Sometimes it just gives dancers a break from the daily grind in the studio. Some rewards I have used are:

- A fun music day (pop music that I don't usually use in class)

- Letting the dancers teach portions of class (this will also show you pretty quickly what concepts are sticking or not)

- Partner day (where the dancers take turns watching each other perform class exercises, maybe even offering positive/corrective feedback)

- A mustache dance day (when each dancer gets to wear a sticker mustache during class. It makes it fun and silly, but we can still do our regular exercises)

- Stickers or stamp charts to fill out as they do things correctly–with little trinkets for students to earn.

Another reward I like to give my students is a compliment day. I offer praise after each exercise and focus on what is going well. This day helps me take a step back and relax in my role as the teacher, and it helps to instill more confidence in my dancers. The gift of confidence is a beautiful reward.

5. Ask questions

One surefire way to engage dancers is to have them figure out the answers. Explain an exercise, then ask questions about it. For example, you could ask your dancers (either individually or as a group) to repeat the counts for you. Maybe ask them to state what the focus of the exercise is. Ask about the energy qualities they will use or what imagery they will think of as they perform the exercise.

Any chance that a dancer has to state their purpose or goal engages them in their learning. Asking questions can prevent your dancers from coasting through class with minimal participation. And if they can't answer your question, you know what you will need to clarify.

6. Use imagery

Physical props aren't always necessary or possible to have in class. Sometimes a particular mental image can spark just as much engagement from your dancers. Imagery is a quick but profound and memorable way to teach a concept. Finding ideas that relate to your students is the key.

Take the movements or techniques you plan to teach and ask yourself if there is a relatable image they can think about. Sometimes I will be going about my day, and something simple will catch my attention. I will notice how something as simple as a spatula lays wide and flat. It scoops up from the bottom and reminds me of what I want to see in my dancers using the floor in tendus (as I mentioned in the "teach with props" section.) I only notice how things relate to concepts I am trying to teach when I have done some lesson planning and thinking ahead. Then I am already in the mindframe to notice similar concepts in unlikely places.

Observe the world around you and note anything that can help your dancers envision what you are asking of them. Think about your dancers and what they need–the inspiration will come. As the inspiration comes, take notes of everything. I often write a quick note on my phone or keep scratch paper on hand.

Some ideas will find their way into your class, and others may not. The key is to start noticing those things that will work as analogies for dance concepts. And the more you recognize and record ideas, the more they will come to you.

One image I have used for relevé is the idea of elevators in the feet (also referenced in Chapter 6.) I ask my dancers to imagine their heel is on an elevator going up, and the ball of their foot is on another elevator right next to it heading down. The relatable mental image of an elevator gets at all the things I want to see: straight up and down with no deviating directions and steady (not jerking) movement.

The image of the parallel elevator going down in the ball of the foot helps create opposition and groundedness in their rélevé/demí-pointe. I have found this particular image very helpful in teaching pointe work.

Another way to help dancers envision how to perform their movement is by recognizing the pathways or patterns they are making. For instance, pas de cheval can be comparable to an eyebrow shape with the round and arched beginning and the tapered lengthening out from there. Frappé translates into a striking image straight and diagonally down like spearfishing. Rond de jambe is an easy half-circle pathway to visualize or like tracing a capital D. Grand battements have weight in their circular swing, similar to a pendulum.

There are a lot of great examples of imagery for dance movement and technical concepts–there are books with pages of ideas. So, here are just a few examples of engaging yet uncomplicated images that I have found to work (some of which we have already discussed):

- **Aligning the hips**: Imagine eyelashes on the front of the hips–keep the eyes open instead of the eyelashes pointing down. Or headlights on the front of the hips–keep them pointing forward. Or suspenders hooked to the front of the hips–lifting up along the torso to keep the hips in alignment.

- **Lengthening the bodies**: Picture a window in the torso–slouching closes the window between the ribs and the hips, and separating the ribs from the hips opens the window nice and wide. Or picture an expanding accordion.

- **Keeping feet balanced** front to back: Imagine the arches are entrances to a small cave and we don't want to close off the opening.

- **Opening shoulders and broadening the chest**: Imagine a bright light shining from the sternum.

- **Elongating the neck and dropping the shoulders**: imagine long dangling feather earrings that you don't want to tickle your shoulders.

- **Engaging lower abdominals**: Imagine slowly zipping tight jeans up to the belly button.

- **Closing the ribs**: Imagine stretchy shoelaces looped between each rib and cinched together in the front.

- **Finding a lift in retiré passé**: Picture the shape of a paper clip and mimic that pathway. Lift along the front of the leg. And at the top of the standing knee, lift a little more to curve around to the back (similar to the curve of a paperclip). Then come straight down on the backside of the leg.

- **Reaching and balancing**: Picture the image of a tightrope walker. They hold onto a long pole to balance while they walk the fine line. Balance is improved when we similarly reach through the space.

- **Peeling the foot** off the floor: Imagine peeling the sticky dots off advertisements in the mail. It stretches and comes up with resistance–pulling and peeling one bit of the goop at a time.

- **Teaching bourrées:** Imagine a spider and how quickly it can travel the length of a room. It is not about the size of the legs but how quickly the tiny legs move. Likewise, bourrée movements are not significant in size–they are just fast and continuous.

Applying imagery in class can be as quick and straightforward as any of those listed. The key is to use a relatable concept (simple to explain and envision) to help your dancers understand something new or unseen to them. They cannot see their bones and muscles, but if they can have an image that helps them engage and align, they can feel what they cannot see.

7. Incorporate literature

Sometimes I use simple stories to introduce a theme for the day. I like to use a short book (I don't want to take a lot of time out of class) that gets the dancers to engage with an idea and begin thinking about something specific. Some fun books I have used are:

- Dr. Seuss's *The Foot Book*[10] for days that we focus on using and shaping the feet correctly,

- Sandra Boynton's *The Belly Button Book*[11] for days that we are focusing on engaging abdominals and central core muscles (the dancers love the silly reminder engage at their "bee-bo"),

- and Sandra Boynton's *Barnyard Dance.*[12] This is a good one for younger dancers because it uses a myriad of movement words like strut, twirl, prance, skitter, swing, slide, scramble, etc. I often read this one to cue movements we have already worked on. It's fun to go through the book and see what movement we will practice next.

Using a simple book to carry a focus throughout class is an excellent way to bring some fun to technique. These are just a few examples.

Another book I have read frequently with older students is Dr. Seuss's *Oh the Places You'll Go.*[13] It is a more extended read, but I often pull it out to read to my classes during times of change or competition. That book has been a great way to open up discussion with students who feel discouraged, maybe after a disappointing audition or at a crossroads with their dance training. It helps the dancers value their journey and think about why they are in class.

Finally, there are several great resource books with great visuals to show dancers how a step is supposed to look and to help them understand how a step is broken down. One of my favorite reference books is *Classical Ballet Technique* by Gretchen Ward Warren. It is full of clear photos of simple and advanced steps broken out into easily understood pieces.

8. Easy sayings and quick cues

Another way to engage dancers is to keep your cues short and catchy. For example, if there is a rhythmic or simple mantra your dancers hear you repeating, they can make quick adjustments with your cues.

One example I love to use comes from Darla Hoover (of Central Pennsylvania Youth Ballet and Ballet Academy East). She uses a fun saying about Mr. **"Tony Heel"** to help with foot shape and rotation in sur le cou de pied (or the coupe position with a foot wrapped around the ankle). The cue "Tony Heel" is to remember to pull back the toe, pull back the knee, and bring the heel forward. **Toe. Knee. Heel.**

This simple saying (after explanation) helps cue many aspects of rotation and foot shape all at once. It's silly and fun and can engage dancers to focus on some critical elements of their technique. My dancers know all about their imaginary dance friend, Tony Heel.

Another one I have used (mentioned in Chapter 4) is **"Practically perfect pliés point over pinky toes."** It helps to cue important aspects of rotation.

I often use the phrase **"down and out"** to cue the image of what the shoulders should feel like in proper technique. They are relaxed down and opened wide in the chest.

Another phrase I use often is **"last one, best one"** when we are nearing the final steps of a combination in technique class. I want my dancers to get that last drive to finish strong.

Simple cues and familiar sayings help your dancers begin to engage with their movement. The most helpful cues are reminders of an image or something you have already discussed as a class, rather than shouting new concepts over the music. With well-placed cues, dancers can make corrections in their technique confidently and begin to correct their practice autonomously.

Thoughts on external adjustments

I am sure we have all done it; we have walked around as our students performed an exercise and adjusted and reshaped different parts of their bodies. However, I have wondered if it is always the best education for my students when I externally change them to specific positions without explanation. It is beneficial for them to understand for themselves how to get to the proper position.

I think external adjustments can be helpful when it is something that you have already discussed, and you use the adjustment as a *reinforcement*. But externally adjusting dancers should not be the first time they are introduced to a concept if we want them to maintain the correction.

This is where the idea of engaging the brain really comes into play. If a dancer can work through the problem themselves, it is more likely to stick. Engaging their own discovery works better than only verbal or only physical corrections. Give your students the tools to correct themselves in various ways. If you are constantly placing them in the position without explanation, you are only fixing them at that moment.

Instead, we want our dancers to know how to put themselves into correct positions on their own. Then our cues and adjustments can better serve as reminders of what they already understand. The key is to give dancers multiple encounters with a concept–teach it verbally, find it physically, enforce with adjustments and verbal cues, etc.

Final thoughts on engaging your dancers

You can use many images, props, and sayings to teach concepts, but the main goal is to engage your students to use their brains and think purposefully. Their learning will be quicker and more meaningful if they are engaged/invested in class.

In writing this book, it was hard to commit to a list of tips because my mental list of useful images constantly shifts and evolves. A stagnant and published list is not sufficient. However, I also think it is important to share my small arsenal of ideas that I have found effective with other teachers to hopefully spark their own ideas of teaching something in an engaging way.

Teaching creatively is a personal thing. Certain mental images and ideas work to engage some students and not others. There are specific ideas here, but they are less of "what to do" and more of an example of "what I do." These tips are intentionally brief and limited. There are so many ways to teach a concept.

Also, do not take for granted that older students have a longer attention span. They still need to be mentally invested, or their dancing will become rote and disengaged. They still need to be challenged with different images and ways of practicing the same exercise.

Do not discount any teaching tool. Any mental imagery or tip can be useful for any level. Older teenagers and adults are not beyond imagining, and younger students can still learn about the unseen muscles of the body. Use all of it in your teaching. What you would typically think is an unfit teaching tool may be the perfect fit for your class.

<u>Summary of Chapter Eight</u>

- Engaging dancers means helping them become invested in their own learning.

- Engaged dancers retain skills and knowledge better than dancers who are just going through the motions.

- Some ways to engage dancers are teaching progressions, teaching in contrast, using props, incorporating reward systems, asking questions, using imagery, incorporating literature, and using easy sayings and quick cues.

- Externally adjusting students can be more effective when it is a reinforcement of something you have already taught.

- Finding ways to engage your dancers will be personal and unique to each class you teach. Dancers of all ages can benefit from imagery and involvement in their own learning.

9

Adapt and Change

Keep some expectations, and be willing to adapt to others

I WAS FINISHING MY college degree when I got a job teaching ballet at a local conservatory. The studio had a set curriculum, and the dancers followed a clear path through the levels. Many of the levels were audition-based. There was a general attitude among the students toward striving to be better. It was built into the culture of the studio. The dancers were goal-oriented. And it was nice being part of a professional environment where most of the students and parents were invested, and they trusted us as teachers.

Around that same time, I got a second job as an assistant ballet teacher at a new high school for the performing arts. A beginning ballet class was a requirement for their dance and musical theater programs, and other students were taking ballet because their friends were in it. So the main class I helped with was a large group of about 50 of those students.

About half of the students in that class appeared uncommitted and not excited about being there. Those kids often didn't come dressed appropriately or show respect for the structure and etiquette of a dance technique class. They were not focused like the students I was used to teaching.

Though I wasn't tasked with the bulk of the teaching, I couldn't help but feel annoyed at first that those students didn't care. I was annoyed that they would disregard rules about dress and etiquette when they were spending their time there anyway.

My eyes were opened to a variety of students throughout that school year.

A couple of years later, I also had a brief stint teaching various dance forms in an after-school club at a junior high (middle school) for a few months. I brought a tiny speaker, and we danced in whatever room or gym was available to us at the school each week. The students had almost no experience in any form of dance.

This experience opened my eyes even further. Many of those students didn't have any dancewear, would show up periodically, and had unavailable parents. It was a low-commitment atmosphere by nature.

I learned something about my teaching between the conservatory, the high school, and the after-school club over those years of educating dancers. I learned that dance is truly for everyone and enthusiastic dance students can be found in somewhat unlikely places. I just had to become more flexible in my approach to see it.

Dancers can have any number of reasons for being in your class. Maybe they have parents who expect them to be there. Perhaps they were curious about trying something new. Or possibly they have goals to pursue dance professionally. Regardless of the reason, they are there in the studio and need to be taught. The *focus* of your teaching is what has to adapt and change to fit their needs.

It's not to say that before those experiences, I thought that dance was only for the "elite" who grew up going to a dance school with a set program. But I came from an atmosphere of high expectations, and many of my peers had professional dance career goals. During my college degree, I was surrounded by those deeply invested and committed to the field of dance. I think I was so caught up in the professionalism of those around me that I forgot that everyone's dance journey looks different.

That was narrow thinking. Everyone's goals for dance are different. I had to change my expectations for my dancers depending on what class I was teaching. I had to figure out why my students were there and teach to those needs.

Don't move the goalposts

An important thing I realized is that I had to adapt expectations but not move the goalposts. Some classes need a strong focus on proper technique. Other groups of students need to focus on putting forth an effort to try new things and show respect before concentrating on the technique. Either way, once I knew what I could ask from my dancers, I held fast to those expectations.

For the dancers in the after-school program, I expected a willingness to try new things and respect for me and their classmates. For my conservatory students, I focused on progressing through the set curriculum, wearing required dance attire, and consistent attendance.

My expectations could not be the same across all of my classes. But my expectations were consistent for each group of students. I often remind myself to set the rules (individual for each class) and not move the goalposts. Here is an example that I have witnessed with my own children:

Our oldest son (8-year-old) often leads when playing together with his younger brother (5-year-old.) He comes up with rules and directs a lot of what happens. Our 5-year-old goes along with it most of the time.

However, sometimes our oldest comes up with a game and then adds or changes the rules part way through playing– usually to his advantage. Those are times when his younger brother becomes upset and pushes back because it's not fair.

If a 5-year-old can recognize the unfairness of changing expectations part way through something, then dance students can recognize it. They deserve that fairness of a consistent through-line.

So do not move your goalposts. This means that if you are teaching a class regularly, lay down the rules in the beginning. Even if you are just conducting a master class or audition, express briefly what you will do and what you expect from the dancers. Let them know what you generally plan to accomplish in that class or semester or year.

Setting expectations will also guide you in your teaching as you go along because you are committed. If you say that you will not allow poor etiquette in class, then stand by that. Enforce and maintain your expectations. Your dancers will rise to the challenge.

I expect a level of etiquette from my dancers of all ages–sort of a baseline of behavior that I expect in the studio. I want all of my students to have self-control and respect for their studio environment. I want them to know I expect them to encourage and respect their classmates. And my dancers know it because I tell them from the beginning. And when I enforce it, they quickly correct their actions because they agreed to that expectation.

Let me share another experience to illustrate the need to adapt your expectations to the needs of your students:

A few years ago, I taught two different groups of dancers–all around the ages 7-9 and all listed as the same level. One class was on Tuesday night, and one class was on Wednesday night. I started the year with an efficient lesson plan that I hoped to use for both groups of dancers. So I was going to get two classes covered for the price of one lesson plan!

The classes turned out to be *starkly* different.

Usually, in a class, I can pick out the one or two students I will need to teach a little differently than the others in the class, and I make minor adjustments as needed. But these two classes were so unlike each other.

The Tuesday group was surprisingly hard-working and attentive for their age. They quickly picked up on the technical concepts for their level. The Wednesday group of girls loved being friendly, goofy, and free-spirited. Of course, all of those traits are acceptable at that young age. Still, I struggled with the latter group for some time because I had different expectations (I was coming from teaching more advanced dancers who didn't need much behavioral direction).

My problem was that I had a plan that I wanted to work for both classes. And the intended curriculum for both classes was supposed to be the same. If the Tuesday class was ready to advance from 3rd to 5th position, then I thought the Wednesday class should move at the same pace.

But as much as I wanted to, I couldn't say the Wednesday class had mastered 3rd position yet. Only when I realized that I needed to take a different approach was our class a lot happier. The dancers didn't have to feel like they were disappointing me for not moving quickly enough.

What did I do differently? I threw my rigid timeline out. I didn't expect my group from Wednesday to be doing the same thing as my Tuesday class anymore. They weren't ready yet. I knew I couldn't move on in good conscience when they had not mastered certain basic concepts.

Their attention span as a whole was shorter. So, I did exercises in shorter bursts and allowed the girls to dance around freely after their four pliés. Of course, I still required them to do it correctly, but I often gave them mental breaks between our class structure.

And what happened when it came time to perform? Both classes performed the same choreography beautifully. They surprised me. I didn't realize that they had been internalizing what I was asking. I didn't know the Wednesday group would pull it together. It was a satisfying moment as a teacher to see our efforts in class come full circle.

Letting go of performance expectations

As discussed in the previous chapter about simplifying, another aspect of adapting expectations goes hand in hand with letting things go.

I have shifted my perspective about performances. Now it is a stress-free joy to come upon concert time. But, it has not always been that way for me.

I decided a few years ago that I would no longer watch critically at a performance of my students. I realized that at concerts and recitals, the prime time for critiques has passed. If I had done my job up to that point, I could allow my dancers the grace of honest mistakes and learning that performing live lends itself to. Their experience on stage is their teacher at that moment. As a result, my tone toward my students changed from "here's what we need to fix and improve" to "look how much you have accomplished and how far you have come!"

Sometimes after my students perform, they come backstage flustered and apologetic for whatever mistakes they made. They say, "I messed up the counts!" or "Did you see me trip on stage?" It seems significant to them, but I genuinely don't see what they are apologizing for more than half of the time. I find joy in seeing their hard work put on the stage and want them to enjoy every second of it. I know how fleeting it can be and how insignificant those mistakes are in the grand scheme of things.

There is a time to step in and critique and a time to keep quiet and let the experience become the teacher. Our students know what they did wrong and feel bad enough when they make a mistake. They are naturally critical of what they are doing. As teachers, we fight our battles in the studio–sweat and work bring a level of satisfaction as a reward. But, there is a different reward on stage–a magic that can only happen under those lights after the work has been put in.

So let your dancers fully experience those moments on stage. Mistakes will happen. Don't take away the joy of raw performance by tainting it with dissatisfaction and critiques. I don't want my students to feel robbed every time they make a mistake on stage. I want them to know they did their best and it is good enough.

Especially with younger students, I think it is more detrimental than helpful to be drilling for perfection up until the curtain call. I think back to my Tuesday/Wednesday class dilemma. Their abilities were different, and at one point in teaching those girls, I had to let my expectations go as we got closer to the concert. It all turned out completely fine, and it may be, in part, because I allowed them the grace to make mistakes.

Establish a foundation against times of uncertainty

Here is one last thought on learning to adapt to your teaching circumstances. At the time of writing this book, a year has passed since the COVID-19 pandemic rocked the world and shut studios down worldwide. At the beginning of the pandemic, I taught three classes that had to move to a synchronous virtual platform to keep teaching. Hundreds of teachers across the world had to do similar things. It was a situation that had never happened before, and it was the ultimate test of adaptation.

Setting a solid foundation at the beginning of the year saved my students and me from losing too much in translation over two-dimensional video. We worked on the same consistent exercises each class before the pandemic, so my students knew exactly what I was expecting—even over a small computer screen.

There is no way I could have known that the pandemic was coming. But we were able to keep moving forward when dance class could no longer be in person. It was because I was able to lay a strong foundation for those girls in their first few months with me.

I also learned to adapt to be more efficient in my teaching. Instead of asking questions for the whole group to blurt out an answer, I asked pointed questions to the dancers by name. That way the entire class could hear, and my students knew I was noticing them individually. I became more efficient with my teaching cues, lectured less, and danced more.

Final thoughts on adapting your expectations

Teaching requires making changes and adjustments depending on the class, day, hour, and even down to the minute. So make the adjustments, but stay firm and transparent in your priorities and expectations.

There are many studio cultures and dynamics to consider. Suppose you teach in lower-income areas where the students can't afford a specific brand of shoes or purchase nice dance attire, or maybe they don't have involved parents to help put their hair up adequately. In cases like those, your goals might differ from a conservatory setting where the culture expects a uniform and a certain amount of time scheduled in the studio. Whatever your studio culture, set appropriate goalposts and don't move them for the group as a whole. But if there are exceptions that need to be made, do that on an individual and personal basis.

As much as these ideas are universal, there are different types of dance schools and students–as there should be. We *want* dancers to feel welcomed from all walks of life. That just means that there are a lot of factors to keep in mind as you strive to meet the needs of the students in your class. Be sensitive to the individual circumstances of the dancers you will encounter. And let these ideas be only a catalyst for your adaptations where needed.

<u>Summary of Chapter Nine</u>

- Every dance class you teach will come with its own unique personality and capabilities.

- Adapt your expectations to fit the individual circumstances of each group you teach.

- Once you understand where your students are coming from, establish classroom expectations early and hold firm to them.

- Let your students enjoy their time on stage, i.e., don't be critical at performance time.

- Clear expectations and classroom procedures will make roadblocks like being separated from your dancers easier to manage.

10

Continue Your Education

Own what you don't know; confidently teach what you do know

IN PARENTING SEMINARS THAT I have attended and parenting books I have read, there has often been discussion about imagining life from your toddler's eyes to understand them. From a young child's perspective, every adult around them is so capable and seemingly faultless.

When my kids struggle with putting their clothes on, I can swoop in and fix it in a matter of seconds. From their perspective, it may seem like I never spill when I pour milk. And I don't struggle to turn doorknobs, and I keep my clothes and face clean when I eat. To them, I am successful at everything I try.

But imagine what they can learn from me if I admit that sometimes I don't have the right words to say and even I have to re-tie my shoes when they come undone.

Similarly, your students are watching you and learning from how you carry yourself and how you approach exercises in class. You know what you are doing when you do a plié because you have done it a thousand times. But when things get difficult for your students, whether they are children or adults, you don't want them to have the impression it was always easy for you. It can be helpful to admit to them the struggles you've gone through. Being vulnerable in front of your students can be a powerful teaching tool.

I have experienced imposter syndrome when I am pushing my limits and trying to improve as a teacher. It can feel like I am in over my head and unqualified to be where I am. However, it has helped me to stay humble and recognize what I don't know. In any case, it's nearly impossible to hide my weaknesses or lack of knowledge in some areas from my students. Students have a way of seeing right through the facade. Instead, be an example of a lifelong learner. Students can learn how to learn by witnessing their teachers' willingness to gain new knowledge.

Continuing education is more than just formal education or certification. It should be an ongoing attitude. Since finishing my dance degree, I have had to proactively seek opportunities for professional development. My education is less formal and more a life pursuit now. Part of bridging the gap between being a student and becoming a teacher is maintaining a connection to learning.

Don't discount anything in your pursuit to improve as a teacher and dancer. Many kinds of experiences form a well-rounded education. Continue to learn about teaching through local workshops, certifications, and adult classes. Push yourself to be creative and watch your peers teach.

Attend workshops

Workshops are a fantastic way to increase your education, gain exposure to different techniques, and keep networking locally or more widely. And they don't have to be with world-renowned teachers. Nowadays, certifications are often accessible online in many cases if you can't travel to the certification workshop in person. I received my Progressing Ballet Technique (PBT) certification locally after a few days of full-time instruction, but they also offer online certification.

Take adult dance classes

Dance classes for adults are helpful because you get to dance and feel the movement yourself again. There have been many times I couldn't find an adult class near me to attend, so I have offered to teach one. And after setting it up, there were almost always other teachers willing to rotate teaching the class. If there isn't time or means to set up an adult class, I have also dropped in to take technique classes with younger/beginner students at our studio. It helps my teaching to put myself in their shoes again and reconnect with learning the basics again from another teacher.

Learn from peers

I watch my peers teach as often as I can make it work. And I have never been turned down when I have asked another teacher to let me observe their class. It doesn't cost anything besides the time to sit in on a class. There was a summer that I lived in another state for my husband's work. One evening I went to a local studio and asked if I could watch a class, and I was able to watch the local professional ballet company in class. It was lovely to observe dancers outside of my local area and feel the sense of community that the dance world offers.

Borrow principles from other exercise forms or retrain yourself

Anything that can teach you how your body moves or keep your mind and body fresh will better inform your teaching. Yoga, Pilates, aerial silks, and floor barre exercises offer a wealth of exercises and insights about the body while utilizing similar skills as technique class. Following videos on YouTube can also be helpful in keeping yourself aware of how dancing feels in your body–which helps maintain awareness of how things might feel for your students. You could go social/ballroom dancing as well and practice working with a partner. Or you could even "take" your own class and practice the class exercises you give to your students. Your body will change as you age, and staying informed about your own body will help you become more aware of different students' needs.

Get out of your bubble

Progression can become stagnant if teachers become "inbred" with their teaching. Sometimes there are regional limitations to how much a dancer can learn because many nearby teachers seem to learn from the same schools and local teachers. Any chance you have to reach outside your local teaching circle is a chance to broaden your students' vision. If you feel your resources are limited where you are, get out of your bubble by traveling to a different studio or speaking to someone who trained in a different geographic or cultural area than you. You will be surprised how willing people are to share their unique experiences with those who sincerely want to listen.

Exploring other parts of the dance world can make you more well-rounded– even if it doesn't directly affect your teaching. For example, you could learn to make or alter costumes, or you could learn about stage production and lighting. There was a time a few years ago when I invested a lot of time in learning how to provide musical accompaniment for ballet classes. I studied a book about dance accompaniment, brushed off the years of piano lessons I had growing up, and collected and practiced pieces of music to use for a ballet class. It helped increase my knowledge and understanding of music for dancers. It also rekindled an old skill and helped me find an interest in a new one–all of which contributed to my dance world experience. The more we know about the dance world, the more we are able to pass on to our students.

Push the limits of your creativity

Jump on opportunities to be creative and keep your mind active. I have planned and submitted many choreography proposals that never made it past the proposal stage. I have been turned down or had the wrong timing when trying to bring some choreographic projects to fruition or land a new teaching position, but I have never regretted making an effort. It has kept my creative ideas flowing–as a teacher and a choreographer. Opportunities to grow ourselves and our craft do not seek us out. We have to do the seeking and be willing to be told "no" at times. Because when we finally hear that "yes," we will be more ready and hungry for the opportunity.

Learning something new may evolve into a tool you will often use. Learning new things will refresh you and save you from burnout with the repetition and sometimes monotony of training techniques–which will, in turn, help your students have fresh ideas to work with to avoid the same pitfalls and fatigue. Sometimes implementing something new in class won't work as you hoped, but that is part of the learning and growing process.

Sometimes when I cook for my family, I find myself in a comfortable rhythm of rotating through the same recipes for a while. I know the ingredients to have on hand, and I know what I am committing myself to when I get started. But every once in a while, I throw out all semblance of order in my kitchen and branch out. I find a new recipe or try to add a new twist to an old recipe. Sometimes it is a wreck, but sometimes it is exciting and successful and becomes a new favorite. It was worth it to educate myself in even the slightest way.

Recognize what you do not know

Students can recognize and respect your contribution while simultaneously seeking more knowledge from other teachers.

Think back to how children view the adults around them. Young children will learn that you are good at many things, but you worked at it and are still learning.

Look at dance from their perspective. Imagine that you are young and you have a teacher you view as a perfect role model. You look up to them, hang on to their every word, and want their approval. Now, imagine down the road you have another great teacher whom you respect and admire–but they have different ideas and opinions than your previous role model. If the first teacher was infallible, how can someone you respect equally have differing opinions? Can they both be right?

The point is there are many ways to teach a class. Every teacher has different strengths. So allow your students to see you admit what you don't know. Let them see the gaps in your knowledge. Then they can allow someone else, or even themselves, to fill in that gap.

Your students will respect you more if they can view you in a positive light despite your imperfections. It is okay to be imperfect. This is a valuable lesson in a field that has thrived on perfectionism for so long.

Your dancers will also gain another lesson from you: that learning is perpetual. Even teachers have things to improve on. My favorite teachers and mentors have been those who are knowledgeable but also human and imperfect at times. It wasn't drastic, but I noticed when they were vulnerable and even took what their students thought into account.

So, how do I show my imperfections as a teacher? I don't go around listing off the things I don't know much about, nor do I put myself down.

Instead, I confidently teach what I have learned. And when the opportunity presents itself, I allow my students to see me learn. When a student asks me a question that I don't know the answer to, I allow myself to be honest and vulnerable enough to admit I don't know. Then I help them find the answer.

I am sure most of my students have seen my little ballet dictionary–the *Technical Manual and Dictionary of Classical Ballet* by .[14] I carry it with my teaching materials and pull it out frequently in class. I have made a conscious choice to carry it because I want my students to know that I don't know everything. I hope my example can encourage my students to be more open to new knowledge.

Additionally, I want my students to know some places they can look if they want to learn more.

If my students ask me something and I don't know exactly how to answer, I will pull out that dictionary or say I need to consult someone else or research a little more and get back to them. Then I make a note of it and I am sure to follow through. There is power in students seeing that you know you don't know everything, but you are willing to learn.

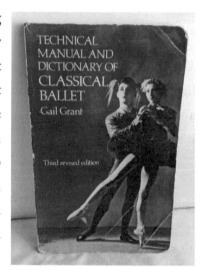

I also often respond to questions from students by starting with the phrase: "from my experience." I want to let them know everyone's experience is different, and my answers come from my perspective.

Final thoughts on continuing your education

I want my students to see me in the process of learning. I want them to be more than just technicians and cookie-cutter dancers. They should be able to find answers for themselves. They should be able to humbly admit what they don't know yet and that mistakes are not an embarrassment. Only then are they truly open to more learning.

And if you receive feedback from parents or fellow teachers, receive it with an open mind. The dance world is small. So take criticism or correction from parents or anyone else with grace.

Imagine what your students learn when you are humble enough to apologize or honest enough to say the words "I don't know."

<u>Summary of Chapter Ten</u>

- Admitting you also need to continue learning sets an example for your students. They can learn from you that it is okay to not have all of the answers.

- All kinds of experiences can provide a more well-rounded education. Some ways to continue learning are attending workshops, getting certifications, taking classes, observing other teachers, and continuing to contribute your own creativity to the dance world.

- You can find a balance between admitting what you do not know and confidently teaching what you have experience with.

11

Love Your Students

See your students as individuals

DO YOU LOVE THOSE you are teaching? Do your students feel your encouragement and support?

Loving our students is what should be at the core of our teaching. Our effort to love our students will make us exceptional teachers, mentors, and coaches who will undoubtedly leave our students better than we found them.

In my observations, there is a pocket of "old-school" teachers who pride themselves in maintaining a "tough love" culture. They want their students to know the harsh realities it takes to succeed in the dance world. From their experience, it can be cut-throat and competitive. And although the dance world may be tough competitively, teaching in a demanding and unforgiving way is neither right nor best.

Dance teaching has to evolve and improve as the dance culture itself has. It seems the traditionally rigid, unforgiving, and discriminatory path to becoming a dancer is becoming more the exception than the rule. We would do well to also adapt our teaching to match. Dance students will benefit more from teachers who behave more like mentors and provide sensitive, thought-provoking instruction.

When I was a younger and inexperienced teacher, I tried to fight all of the battles and expected everything from my students. It was exhausting, and my students were missing my approval and the validation that their work was enough. Now I try to fight for what matters most. I expect my students to show up with their work ethic and willingness to try. I have replaced my expectation of daily perfection with valuing more of a growth mindset. I try to expect daily effort, not just success.

I am not saying we cannot ask a lot of our students. Discipline and focus are a big part of progressing in any skill. We should require precision in the basics and not allow dancers to practice techniques incorrectly. But *how* we correct and ask for more makes a difference.

I am glad to see the world move more toward accepting environments and away from harassment and discrimination. I feel a need to call out attitudes in the dance world that cultivate unhealthy competition, lack of mutual respect, and a sergeant/soldier relationship rather than a teacher/student relationship. Yes, there is a place for competition. But we would do well to not overvalue competition above dancer wellness.

We can create environments where our students feel accepted and valued for who they are as individuals. Ensuring our students feel safe has just as much value in our teaching as any lesson we can teach about technique. We can foster mental health in our dancers and not be solely concerned with their physical abilities.

Showing love to students is challenging at times

Chances are that you are already genuinely invested in helping your students succeed and you care deeply about them. But some students are challenging, and some days it is hard to teach with love. There have been times when I have not loved or noticed my students enough. I am still learning to be an effective teacher every time I step into the studio, and my students have had a front-row seat to my flaws as a teacher.

One experience, in particular, leaves me wishing I could go back and change the way I approached a student. The student's mother contacted me as we were nearing the end of the dance year. She expressed how her daughter used to love coming to dance, but she no longer enjoyed it. This student felt singled out and teased by me that year.

I was heartbroken to hear that. I recognized some of the things the student's mother said I did, and I felt horrible that this student felt picked on. It was unintentional and definitely not malicious, but I was not aware of this student enough to notice. It was mostly due to some miscommunication.

After that information was shared with me, I fixed things with that student and her mother. But the time had already passed. The dance year was nearly over.

So, I write this chapter in humble contrition. I never want a student to leave my class again feeling less valued or respected. And though I am sure I continue to make mistakes in this area, I am consciously working to improve.

The following are ways I try to love my students:

1. Picture students in the future

At the beginning of the year, I often hand out paper and pens to my older students on the first or second day of class. I ask them a few questions to get to know them and to help them set goals. For example, I usually ask what they want to be when they grow up, what other hobbies they enjoy, and why they are in dance class. I keep the sheets of paper with their answers to refer back to them throughout the year. I am always surprised and intrigued by the responses I receive in this exercise.

Many of my students just love to dance, but they don't always see themselves doing it their whole life. It makes me step back and ask myself: Did I even know what I wanted to be when I was younger? The answer probably shifted with each new year–even when I was committed to dancing.

I have had students who want to be doctors, veterinarians, school teachers, writers, swimmers, artists, mothers, fathers, etc. But right now, they love to dance, so they show up and put in the work during this stage of their life. There is a place for each of those students in my class.

The truth is that most dancers will not become full-time dance professionals. Not all dancers come to class intent on becoming professional in the dance field either–even if they are serious students at an advanced level.

We should never assume that all students have the same intentions and goals. The number of students you have coming into your class is equal to the number of life trajectories that will come out of your class. Each dancer's path is unique–but you will have an opportunity (however small) to help shape that path.

Does that mean I focus my energy on those students who want to go on to have a career in dance? Of course not. If we only taught dance seriously to those who had intentions to become professional, we would be neglecting all the students who enjoy dancing for fun in public schools, trying dance as a hobby, and those who want the benefits of dance training without the lifetime commitment.

But while they are in your class, what difference can you make for them while they are there? What encouragement and direction can you give?

I have learned to stop looking at dancing as a singular life path for my students–and myself included. Dance does not need to be your students' life path, no matter how passionate they are about it. Passions change and evolve. They grow and fade. I have had seasons in my life when dance has been in the forefront and seasons when it has taken a back seat to other things. But the lessons I learned as a dancer underlie everything that I pursue.

So rather than viewing your dancers on the singular path or trajectory to being stellar dancers, try to view your class as one chapter of their life. What do you want to write in their memories during this chapter? Asking this question always helps me view my students as individuals with their own futures. I look to the future, and it allows me to teach them to the best of my ability today.

Any dancer can eventually find their way in the dance world if they want it. Whether as a professional performer, teacher, choreographer, costume designer, etc., they will see doors open if they are willing to work for it. And those who lose interest, aren't fully invested, or aren't remarkably talented may eventually weed themselves entirely out of dance in favor of other hobbies and interests at some point. It is their journey to decide.

So, figure out why your students are there. Do they have goals to dance professionally? Do their parents want them there? Do they enjoy dancing casually? Do they like the social aspect of dancing with friends? Are they unsure of what they want?

Then encourage the dreamers and strive to inspire those who don't know their dream quite yet. For those dancers who are unsure, you have an opportunity to instill a love and appreciation for dance. Where there may only be a scheduled obligation to come to class, you can plant a desire and a dream and teach invaluable life skills like respect and etiquette.

And where it is applicable, keep the parents and guardians involved. Send home updates. This may sound time-consuming, but it pays in the end, to give students feedback even before they ask for it—and not just dancing feedback. Tell them and their parents what you enjoy about them. Reaching out to their families is one way to look beyond your students in class and see them as individuals with their own aspirations.

Even if you are just coming in as a guest teacher, try to *see* your students. They have hopes and desires. They have doubts and feel unsure of what their path holds for them. They have a life outside of the studio. Create space for them in the present. Keep a broad perspective for your students and teach them to view themselves similarly.

And when thinking of the future of your dancers, ask yourself what success really means. Then train your students to value their personal gains and the day-to-day wins. Success doesn't have to just look like a few minutes on stage, a scholarship, or a professional contract. With hard work, those things can, and will, come around to those who stick with it and work hard.

To gain some perspective, sometimes I read to my more mature dancers this portion from Theodore Roosevelt's famous speech "The Man in the Arena":

> "It is not the critic who counts; not the man who points out how the strong man stumbles, or where the doer of deeds could have done them better. The credit belongs to the man who is actually in the arena, whose face is marred by dust and sweat and blood; who strives valiantly; who errs, who comes short again and again, because there is no effort without error and shortcoming; but who does actually strive to do the deeds; who knows great enthusiasms, the great devotions; who spends himself in a worthy cause; who at the best knows in the end the triumph of high achievement, and who at the worst, if he fails, at least fails while daring greatly, so that his place shall never be with those cold and timid souls who neither know victory nor defeat."[15]

I share that quote with them because I want my dancers to know the rewards that come from the process, not just the outward achievement of public recognition or notoriety. They deserve the credit and kudos for their daily work in class. Their personal growth is a worthy byproduct of their effort, not only the praise or trophy they receive from some external source.

Dancers can burn out from the effort, struggle, and roadblocks they will inevitably encounter. Encourage your dancers to slow down and refocus their efforts at home and in the studio. Eric Franklin, in his book *Dance Imagery for Technique and Performance,* says, "When dancers make slow or little progress, it is because they are recycling their problems. To progress, they must make a full stop, noticing whether what they are doing is their best work and, if not, try something new."[16] This means that when our students struggle, whether technically or emotionally, it is our job to be willing to help them take a step back and reevaluate their goals and intentions with dance. Maybe they need to rekindle or find their desire to put in the work.

2. Balance praise and correction

Know when to correct and when to concede. As discussed earlier, we know there is the best time for critiques (and it's not the day of the performance). However, corrections need to happen. Discipline and a willingness to learn are essential in dance, and it carries over into many aspects of life and whatever your students will decide to do in their future.

Inevitably and continually, you will need to correct your dancers. So how do you critique your students with love rather than create a discouraging laundry list of things they are doing wrong?

A few years ago, my husband and I attended an insightful parenting workshop by Ralphie Jacobs, a parenting educator and the owner and founder of *Simply on Purpose.*[17] The workshop was all about positive parenting. One thing that stood out to me was the 8:1

Principle. The idea of this principle is to have eight positive interactions for each negative interaction. This handy guideline aims to guard against children feeling shut down or becoming completely unresponsive to correction. It's an interesting thought which we will come back to.

When I was in college, I worked as a supervisor in the university institutional research call center. One of the main parts of my job was performing quality interviews one-on-one with the callers. I tried to begin with what they were doing well in each interview. I thought they would find me more approachable and be more receptive to what I had to say if I complimented them first.

One particular employee mentioned that she appreciated how I gave positive feedback first in an interview. She said that she recognized my job was to offer corrections, but she appreciated that I did not skip over the opportunity to build her up as well.

I have tried to apply these ideas in some way to my teaching. But as idyllic and lovely as it sounds, it is also daunting to try and compliment frequently. 8:1 is a wide ratio. There is still work to do in class, and we can't waste too much time feeding egos and filling the room with flowery but overblown compliments.

However, it makes a difference for your dancers to know that you see their good qualities and what needs improvement. If you acknowledge the good they do, your students can understand that their hard work isn't for nothing. It doesn't always have to be eight to one, but it is something to think about.

One way to help you pump the breaks before offering too many corrections is to think about connecting before correcting. Do the early work to lay the foundation of respect for your students. And at the moment before correction, view your students wholly, not just their weaknesses that need correction. Striking a balance between praise and correction is the goal–and sometimes one is needed more than the other. Too much praise or too few corrections can be detrimental to progress. So be sensitive to that balance.

When people are willing to see the best in me, I am more inclined to give of myself and be vulnerable. If someone can see the good in me, I feel safe. When dancers feel the same and give more of themselves, it allows them a safe space to progress as an artist.

Even for those challenging students (we've all had those), it is good practice to look for the best in them. I am not talking about praising how they use their feet if they don't use their feet well. But praise them for their gentle port de bras or attention to timing mingled with the necessary corrections. Praise them for whatever it is they are doing well.

If you briefly offer praise for even the most minor things, your students will be more open to wanting feedback from you. At the very least, they will *really* get into doing that port de bras for you because you noticed it and mentioned how you liked it. They will want to do more of what you love and praise them for. I think it's human nature to want to do the things that bring us positive feedback–even recognition and praise.

Obviously, coddling students is different from considering their needs, feelings, and perspectives. We don't need to indulge, but we do need to consider our students.

Complimenting and praising can open the door for more learning. It will build a relationship of respect as your students learn they can trust you and are not discouraged by you. We don't ever want to be a stumbling block for our students–there is already enough difficulty in dance training. If you look for and praise the good, then you will see more of it.

3. Observe more, correct less

Those who know me may notice I am often too quick to share my opinion. I have looked back on many conversations wishing I had talked less and listened more. I am working on being more aware of it in my personal life.

I am working on it in the studio too. Sometimes I just need to see my students, stop my agenda, and just observe. How can I evaluate where they stand in their progress if I don't acknowledge how far they have come? This is where the balance of critique and compliments also comes into practice.

Sometimes you should step in and correct. Sometimes you should observe and wait.

Slowing down and taking time to observe helps us to avoid judging wrongly. Sometimes slowing down and not making rash corrections will help us more clearly see a student who is having a particularly challenging day or a student who is actually working hard but still struggling to understand a concept.

I have been on the receiving end of this type of mindful mentorship. There was a time when I was dancing in college, and one day I went to class soon after receiving some shocking and devastating news. It was an emotional experience for me to go to class and dance, and I am not sure how well I performed any of the exercises. My professor came up to me and simply asked if I was doing okay. It was difficult to hold back tears, and I felt relief knowing that my teacher saw my struggle and didn't put my technical performance above my personal needs that day. I just needed to dance as an outlet without worrying too much about the perfection of my technique.

It makes a difference to know you are not just a body in a classroom.

Many of my colleagues and mentors say that, if you see a mistake, stop class and correct it, so it doesn't become a habit. I love this idea–practicing doesn't make us better unless we practice better. We need correction and guidance to improve. However, if you are constantly correcting, have you evaluated if those are really the corrections your dancers need to hear? And what should your dancers focus on changing first?

It circles back to simplicity and focus, as described in Chapter 7. If we have a focus and clear expectations, our corrections are more intentional and less overwhelming.

I try to let the critiques help my students discover what works for them. If I genuinely engage my students in class, they will be receptive and hungry for more guidance to figure out the puzzle. My feedback is best received when I err on the side of direction more than criticism.

We sometimes hide demeaning criticism under the disguises of "tough love" and "constructive criticism." We let them masquerade as doses of the "real world." But in reality, it is an immature abuse of power to belittle students to help them improve.

When we choose to correct our students, it should come from a place of mutual respect–not from a place of power to produce compliance. If we aim to fix everything under the sun, each correction loses its impact and can feel like a list of personal flaws to the student.

The key is offering critiques with consistent thought and intention towards the greater goal–building dancers who are autonomous and confident.

This idea comes with a caveat. I still have to decide where I will not budge. It goes back to keeping the goalposts stationary. Not every moment of class can be full of praise and free reign. Some things need to be said clearly and not glossed over. That is where an unwavering daily focus comes in. It is different from "tough love."

And the way you observe your dancers will differ depending on who you teach. It will vary by level. In a class of 4-year-olds, I can't sit on a stool in the corner and just observe. However, if I have established a routine, and the students know the exercises and what I expect, I can mentally step back and watch before moving forward.

And if I lay out my expectations at the beginning of each rehearsal/class/workshop/year, I must stick with them. Then my dancers will likely accept corrections more quickly and not perceive them as personal attacks.

I have to do this with my children too. If my husband and I tell them that at 7 pm we need to start getting ready for bed, they know what to expect at 7 pm. But if we don't say anything about bedtime until 7 pm and still expect them to get ready for bed calmly and quickly, it suddenly introduces new expectations. It never goes over well. I can learn a lot from watching my young kids. Our expectations are best met when we have clearly communicated them.

Dance students are also impressionable and deserve to know what we expect from them. Therefore, we want our corrections to be focused on helping them discover how to make the steps work for them. Let your corrections be a reinforcement of your focus for the day.

Corrections don't need to fix everything at the moment. That would be too much. Instead, correct the few things you're focusing on that day.

Laying out expectations also allows your students to respect you as their teacher. Students can tell when their teachers are uncommitted to enforcing something in technique and behavior. They will push the line to find the boundaries of what behavior is allowed. Love your students, but be confident and firm in your expectations.

4. Do not praise or discourage body shapes

While we are talking about praise and correction, it is valuable to remember to compliment your students' *efforts* and not their physical traits.

More and more, I see an emphasis on athleticism and intelligent dancing. This view is refreshing. Those qualities are essential because they go beyond the fixation with body type. At least things are moving that way with more crossovers of dance genres and professional companies that perform all sorts of repertoire. As a firm believer that dance can be for anyone, I think this is important to foster in your own studio space.

Body shaming can happen to anyone in the dance world—male or female. And though I am not a qualified therapist, I'd like to address it through my own lens of experience.

It can be hard to encourage all body types in a field that has glorified a thin body aesthetic for so long. I have found myself at times fighting against feeling ashamed of the curves I see in my own body. It is a cycle we need to break. As teachers, we need to shift the focus away from the imaginary "perfect dancer body" and encourage a more holistic approach.

When I was pregnant with one of my boys, I remember being anxious to announce to my students and their parents as soon as possible that I was expecting. I hate to admit it, but part of my anxiousness was rooted in a fear that they had noticed I had gained weight. I wanted to tell them I was pregnant, so they had an explanation for seeing me getting larger.

I had to stop myself and ask if that is the kind of example I should give my students. They deserved a confident teacher who was comfortable in her own body. That attitude could then carry over to them. I realized I didn't want any body-shaming thoughts to come from me as their teacher. Nor did I want to foster those unhealthy feelings in myself.

I also realized I could still find and demonstrate a neutral pelvis and proper skeletal alignment even with the added weight of a baby and the associated body alignment changes. That realization only further solidified in me that anyone can find a way to demonstrate proper dance techniques–regardless of their shape or size.

Thankfully, I grew up dancing in a studio environment that, despite its flaws, was not openly hung up on body size or shape. I am grateful my teachers did not knowingly or regularly pressure me to make my body be a certain way. Of course, this is not everyone's experience, but you can help make your studio a safe place for your students.

I believe any teacher who is honestly working to give their students their very best wants to teach the whole student. We don't shape bodies to dance; we shape people who dance. Therefore, it matters how we address our students' bodies. And it matters how we address our bodies in front of them. We don't want to inadvertently pass insecurities about our body image onto our impressionable students.

So how do I share body positivity and avoid body shaming with my students? One way is to watch how I cue certain aspects of their dancing.

There is definitely a strong history of pointed body-shaming and discriminatory practices in the dance world. There is a lot of focus in dance on the body's shape, particularly the abdomen. Unfortunately, though, I think some teachers wrongly focus too much on "sucking in the tummy" without enough connection to the reason behind it.

Some of the emphasis on pulling in the abdomen is meant from a good place. Chapter 3 talked about alignment as the first constant, and it is clear that correctly engaging the abdominals can make or break alignment. However, I think there aren't enough teachers who spell out the reason for cueing "pull in your tummy" or "suck in your belly button." And without knowing why their teacher is saying that, dancers are left wondering what is wrong with the shape of their tummy, among other things.

This misconception is where the change has to happen. Your students still need to engage their abdominals. But you do not need to tell them to suck in their belly until it looks flat. Instead, teach them to look at their skeletal alignment and see how their bones stack up. Look intentionally at the muscles and skeleton inside, not purely the shape of the abdominals on the outside. When I cue dancers to remember to engage their abdominals, I almost always pair it with a cue to find their pelvic alignment. I want them to make the connection between abdominals and alignment—not abdominals and thin aesthetics.

The same thing goes for telling dancers to tighten or squeeze their glutes. I received this cue several times growing up. I didn't know if there was a problem with the shape of my glutes or if I was doing something wrong.

Dancing as an adult, I realized that the focus my teachers placed on my glutes was supposedly to help me use my rotators. It was not a helpful cue and mostly left me wondering if there might have been something wrong with my dancing or my body itself. Additionally, I know now that my glutes will not be the primary driver in my hip rotation. They are a relatively small part of it.

So cueing your dancers to pull in their tummy or squeeze their glutes are examples of misguided cues or incomplete ideas. They are not as effective as teaching proper alignment and rotation.

If you teach concepts, rather than specific body shapes, your students will understand why things like engaging their abdominals and glutes are essential. It is more than "sucking in" to appear skinny or pulling in the glutes for a flat behind. They will understand that using their abdominals helps align their hips and rotation comes from the rotation in the hips right below the glutes. Teach from a functional standpoint and not necessarily an aesthetic one.

Most importantly, the only talk about our dancers' bodies should be brief and untethered to a discussion of body shape and size. We would also do well to discourage any bodily abuse, verbal or otherwise, in our students. To do that, we can model an appreciation and love of our bodies for all that they are capable of. We should simply encourage our dancers to take care of their bodies for health and longevity. No specifics are needed beyond that.

5. Address students by name

It may sound small, but one easy way to show respect and love to your students is to use their names at least once each class.

No dancer wants to come to class, put in the time, and feel like they leave class without being noticed. Dance class can be a wonderful place of belonging and acceptance, and something as simple as using a student's name and looking them in the eyes can create that belonging. Using your dancers' names also helps them become more engaged in what you ask of them.

Sometimes you teach dancers who you don't know personally. They may be in a new class, a workshop, or an audition you are teaching. But you still want to view and evaluate each dancer. There are always those dancers who easily stand out, but each dancer needs personal attention and feedback. Each dancer needs to be seen and their needs considered in each class.

So even if you don't know them by name, you can address each dancer individually as you go around the room. Look them in the eye. Or ask individual dancers to demonstrate things they are doing well to the rest of the class. A single moment of personalized attention can positively impact a dancer for years.

Final thoughts on loving your students

Some students' behaviors and attitudes are difficult to tolerate. As your fellow teacher, I salute you in solidarity along with every other teacher out there. Consider yourself validated!

I think the same concepts here can help with problem students. Be consistent, offer encouragement, and talk with parents when possible. Often I have discovered that parents and guardians will understand your viewpoint, and they can help you develop a plan to help their particular child. Of course, they want their child to succeed, and in many cases, they don't even know their child is having problems until you reach out.

One year I had a student who struggled with focusing, and she often disrupted the class with chatting and silliness. So I reached out to her mother for some help. Her mom got back to me with a discipline plan for her daughter. I followed the plan and it improved her behavior. I would never have thought of it before, and to be honest, I have never used the idea on any students since. It was specific for that dancer and helped her immensely for the rest of the year. But I would never have known to try something different without reaching out to her mother for help.

If you work with a team of teachers for the same dancers, you can collaborate with the other teachers to help with problem students. Sometimes dancers work well with certain teachers and not with others. Using other teachers as a resource can help you find a better way to reach a struggling student.

Most of all, create a safe environment for your dancers—especially the difficult ones. They may realize what you did for them later down the road, even if they don't see it or appreciate it now.

The culture where you teach affects your efforts to create a safe place for your dancers. I have taught in some studios where they seem to value militant teachers and unhealthy competition. Those kinds of toxic environments may turn out technicians, but they rarely produce well-rounded and resilient dancers without consequences. It can cause unintentional lasting harm in the way those students view their bodies or how they gauge success. A dancer's success does not need to be dependent on pushing their body to harmful limits or beating another dancer out of a role.

In contrast, I have also taught in studios where the culture is to value the dancer's well-being as a whole. As a result, there is mutual respect between directors, teachers, students, and parents. That kind of environment breeds dancers who succeed beyond the studio.

Find a studio where you can be a part of the culture of building up rather than tearing down. Find a studio that you and your dancers can call home.

Summary of Chapter Eleven

- The way you teach your students does not have to only follow a pattern of "tough love" in order for your dancers to be successful. You can balance your love for your students with your need to correct and teach them.

- While some students are challenging to teach, there are some tips that can help with showing love to all students. These tips include picturing students in the future, balancing praise and correction, observing more, avoiding body shaming, and addressing students by name.

- It is easier to foster a love for students when you teach at a studio with a culture that actively values that relationship.

- Through loving your students, you can avoid personal regrets and leave a legacy of students who feel valued.

12

Your Purpose

Why do you teach?

My husband works as a technical architect. His job is to create and program systems for data that will work indefinitely with little to no variance or interference. It should mostly run itself, with only a few tweaks as needed. My husband told me that he knows he has done his job well when he can set up a system and leave it–only checking in when there are issues.

Teachers are not programmers.

Teaching is not a "set it and forget it" profession. Education is fluid and changes with the students who walk in the door. It's an emotional investment.

Recognize, but don't be afraid of, the weight and responsibility of being a teacher. You are in the position to shape and influence your students' future.

I wish I had always taken advantage of that responsibility to help shape my students' future and envision a broader scope for them. I would have sweated less about the small things and made more of a conscious effort to focus on where I could see my students by the end of the year and beyond. But I do my best to show my students how I am human and show them I am trying.

While you do have to adapt from class to class, it is possible to create a system of concepts, or mental bullet points, to be a more effective and intentional teacher. I hope we have covered many of those in the pages of this book. Effective teaching does not need to feel overwhelming.

When I think of my purpose as a teacher, the concept behind the phrase "do no harm" comes to mind. Doctors take an oath and promise to do no harm to individuals first and foremost. Then patients and doctors have a mutual understanding that what their doctor suggests and practices is in their patient's best interest to the best of their ability as a doctor. Similarly, we should vow to "do no harm" and create a safe space for our students to progress.

I want to leave my students better than I found them. That thought guides all of my teaching. And when I plan for my classes, I review that goal and ask myself if I am doing just that.

We don't have to give an inspirational discourse or lecture each class, but we should keep our goal in mind. That could mean advancing our dancers' technique. It could also mean teaching them perseverance and hard work through pushing through the difficulties of dance training. We lay our expectations and set a plan and trajectory. Then, when we teach, we keep that safe place and see how we can improve our dancers from there.

Of all the questions you could ask yourself, it all comes down to the guiding and overarching question: How do your students feel at the end of class? Do they feel empowered, accomplished, and challenged? Or are you inadvertently making them feel small, criticized, and frustrated? I'm sure we'd all like to aim for the former.

The impact of a teacher

Sometimes the slightest comment can stick with your dancers for years to come. Many years later, I still remember some things my teachers emphasized and ingrained in me.

One teacher told me to always be aware of the shape of my feet. She showed me what a sickled foot looked like and how to correct it. She said to notice it and correct it when I am sitting in my chair at school or in the car and even to notice the shape of my feet when I lay down in my bed. It stuck with me, and I have been doing that for as long as I can remember. I still find myself fixing the shape of my feet in the most unlikely settings. It is subconscious now and makes me chuckle when I realize what I am doing even so many years later. I'm amazed by how one piece of advice, one time, has remained with me for so many years and even affects the way I fall asleep!

So, exercise caution when giving corrections. You don't know what will leave a lasting impression on your students–good or bad. You are not aiming to turn out clones and technicians. Instead, you are creating a generation of dancers–moving artists who feel and create on stage and off. Your words and attitude have a lasting impact.

I am learning that lesson through my kids. I do not send them to school, only hoping they learn the alphabet and how to do math. I also want them to have a sense of belonging. I want them to learn social skills. I expect them to be taught values and to be valued. And above all, I hope and pray that their teachers respect them and influence their lives positively.

It is the same for dance class. Being a teacher comes with a great purpose—we are creating more than just dancers. The guiding reason for anything we do in class is centered around leaving our students better off and not just teaching some movements of the body. And if you look back on those teachers who left an impression on you, you already know this.

Through our teaching, we build up people. Requiring persistence creates determined individuals. Asking our students to respect us, the studio space, and their classmates will teach them to have respect outside of the studio too. Teaching dancers to work for something and see it come to life through their personal efforts gives them the gift of true satisfaction. The studio is a workshop for life lessons, not only building muscle and increasing flexibility. These are the types of lasting lessons they can gain from us, and we are more fulfilled in our mission as a teacher when we remember to teach those lessons.

Your dancers spend a lot of time with you, whether one hour a week or ten hours. Imagine the hopes their parents or guardians have for them. They are entrusting their kids to you for a time. Adult students are likewise entrusting their time to you. It can be overwhelming, or it can be empowering to realize the impact you can have as their teacher.

Look more fully now at how you approach your students. Facilitate a strong basis in their technical training in the best environment you can give them.

Teaching is not meant to be solely altruistic and self-sacrificial. Dance education can bring deep satisfaction and joy beyond helping our students become better dancers. Teaching dancers who can become life-long friends is a reward. There is hardly anything more fulfilling than growing something and seeing it come to fruition. We are growing dancers into thriving artists and contributors to the human race.

Burnout

Though there is immense joy in teaching, sometimes teaching can become too much to carry. Yes–teaching can be rewarding, fulfilling, and inspiring! Thank you notes from dancers, little gifts, and witnessing your dancers discover and succeed are rewards from teaching. But being a teacher can be equally discouraging, exhausting, and stretch us too thin. It is easy in those times to feel slack in our confidence and to feel burnt out.

When we experience fatigue and lack of motivation to continue teaching, we need to recognize it and make the necessary changes in our lives. Otherwise, we are half-hearted and ineffective as teachers.

At times in the past, I have felt the pull to step back from teaching, but I have ignored it because I have been afraid that I won't be able to come back if my foot is "out the door." And as teachers, we may worry that we can only keep our teaching skills if we don't continually practice them.

But only in recent years have I realized that if I am invested and caring as a teacher, the door for teaching opportunities is never fully closed.

After I had my third son, I knew it was time to take a break from teaching and spend time with my little family for a season. Despite my hesitation to step back from such a large part of my life, I found that time away to be precious and renewing. It was almost a sacred choice to give more attention and balance to those parts of my life outside of dance.

I was able to mentally reframe my focus on my family and feel a refreshed perspective on how to approach teaching going forward. Instead of dreading or feeling drained in the studio, I now feel a renewed sense of purpose. I am not sure I would have found that if I hadn't taken a step back.

Taking on less, or even taking a pause, might be a necessary step in rekindling your joy in teaching.

It is important to remember that dance does not have to be a continuous life path—for our students or for ourselves. There are chapters. There are hills and valleys. Sometimes you can handle the pressure of teaching many regular classes, and sometimes you can only take on one or two.

If taking a complete break from teaching is not possible for you, maybe for income needs or losing a teaching position, there are other ways to avoid total burnout. You could request to teach an entirely different level or genre from what you are currently teaching. Sometimes when I have felt stretched too thin, moving to teach new students, teaching virtually from my home, or even teaching a different genre of dance has saved my sanity.

Our confidence as a teacher can break as well. Sometimes, even with our continued effort and striving, we have students who continue to struggle, or we may feel like our teaching doesn't make a difference. In those times, I try to remind myself that if I am doing my best, then that is enough. The fruits of my labor may not be fully realized until later.

If you find yourself getting burned out, I also recommend rekindling your original love for dance–whatever that means for you in your current stage of life. It helps me to watch another teacher I admire or to take a feel-good dance class for myself. Sometimes rekindling my love for dance just means reconnecting with my body through slow, focused stretching, breathing, and yoga-like exercises.

We have to keep ourselves functioning and inspired if we also want to be able to inspire our students.

Going forward

I felt some hesitation in writing this book and presenting it to teachers who would inevitably have different needs and experiences with their students. But I realized that I was writing it in part because I also wanted to solidify more of these ideas in myself. I wanted to be a better teacher to those dancers I had the privilege of influencing.

We all fall short at times. But the desire to improve ourselves and our dancers makes our pursuit worthwhile.

We know our dancers can live more fulfilling lives outside the studio when they learn the proper lessons inside the studio. We know it because we have lived it. We have put in the work, sweat, and tears to get to where we are. As teachers, we have stayed with dance because of what it has done for us. So let us also resolve to give our students the best experience we can.

It may be easy to think: we are *just* dance teachers. Our influence ends when our dancers leave the building. But dance class is about more than dance. Dancing is much more than movement with rules. The studio is a place to learn perseverance, creativity, and taking risks.

Dance class is a place of tremendous growth and achievement for those who put in the work. Dance helps our students become better people.

And will all of these methods consistently produce the best dancers in the world? Maybe not. But I would argue that the better dancers are those who are engaged in their learning and valued for who they are. Those dancers will feel more deeply and know how to trust themselves and their purpose–not only as dancers–but in anything else they choose to pursue. They will have longevity because they will find a way. They will be resilient.

Dance is meaningful. It is an art of expression and helps us feel alive and accomplished. It brings joy to others. I love walking into the studio and feeling at home. There is something about the wide open space–open for creativity and possibilities. It feels right to be there. Let us help our students to feel the same contentment and reassurance that the time they spend with us in the studio matters.

Let's leave our students better than we found them–what a beautiful and memorable legacy that will be.

<u>**Summary of Chapter Twelve**</u>

- Teaching is an involved profession–you can't just set it and forget it.

- The things we say and do as teachers can have a lasting impact on our students.

- Teaching dance can bring joy, but it can also cause burnout. Avoiding burnout can look like taking a break, teaching different genres or levels of dancers, and rekindling our personal love for dance.

- Even though we are *just* dance teachers, we have the ability to help shape our students' futures. We can leave a legacy of inspired students when we teach your students in a well-rounded way. We can inspire our students to work hard in the studio and beyond.

Acknowledgments

It would be impossible to write this book without acknowledging my own numerous dance teachers throughout the years. The ideas here have evolved while learning at the feet of those accomplished mentors. So to my teachers: Your impact is evident in the way I live my life. You have taught me perseverance in the studio. You encouraged and challenged me. You were always my idols—the people I wanted to be like when I grew up. Thank you.

Thank you to my students over the years. You have shaped me and been patient with me and my flaws. You have been the guinea pigs for my best and worst ideas in the studio. I am grateful most of all that I can still call many of you my friends—even as you have grown into adulthood. It is a joy to see you grow and flourish in your own lives.

This book would be a mess of notes and incoherent thoughts without my willing readers Tanja, Corinne, and Shayla. I want to thank each of you for your feedback and generosity even in the infant stages of drafting. You saw the potential through the mess. You willingly gave me valuable advice. I will be forever grateful for the time you spent reading and offering thoughtful and unique insight from your perspectives. You were each kind and gracious—reassuring me that I had something to offer. Thank you for your encouragement and enthusiasm. I value my relationship with each of you, and I am so grateful to know you.

Thank you to Steph for creating the kind of studio environment that I always wanted to be a part of. You have created a place where I love to teach and dancers love to come learn. Thank you for letting me learn to be a teacher at your studio. You are generous, genuine, and kind. The dancers who have come through those studio doors probably don't know how lucky they are to be TDC dancers.

Thank you to Ella and Abby for modeling for this book. Your beautiful technique and clean lines demonstrate so well. You even make demonstrations of wrong techniques look good! Thank you for workshopping with me to get the best photos. You are both mature and talented beyond your years and I am blessed to have worked with you. You both have great futures ahead of you in the dance world and beyond.

Thank you to Sarah. From the moment I saw a sample of your work I knew I wanted to work with you. You took all of my random thoughts and ideas and made sense of them to create the beautiful cover for this book. Your artwork is amazing and deserves to be seen. Your depictions of dancer anatomy and form are beautiful. All of the emails back and forth paid off! Thank you so much for working with me.

Thank you to Natalie. There are a hundred things I could thank you for! Who would have thought that those giggly girls at summer dance camp years ago would reunite again over publishing a book? I am in awe at the timing of us finding each other again. You are an editing wizard and a kind critic. You not only helped fix my writing to make it more clear, but you taught me throughout the process. Thank you for taking this project on with so much enthusiasm. You spent so much time behind the scenes researching, working, and marketing. I am full of gratitude for the chance to work with you.

Thank you to my parents—for the years of investment in dance lessons, costumes, and concerts. You always encouraged me and supported me. I am not sure if you knew how those dance lessons would shape my life, but I am forever grateful for them. You are some of the most generous people I know. I am blessed to be your daughter.

To my children. If I can teach anyone well, I want it to be you. Thank you for teaching me patience and forgiveness. To my boys, thank you for always being excited to visit the studio and enjoy dance parties with me. Your enthusiasm for life equally invigorates me and exhausts me and mostly brings me joy. I am excited to see the men you will become. And to my daughter. You were born in the middle of the process of writing this book, and I am so happy you came to our family. One day you will accomplish beautiful things.

And to Chandler. From the night that I said I wanted to write a book, you never questioned me. You have fully supported and encouraged me. Thank you for reading, asking the hard questions, laughing at the clichés in my writing, and listening to me talk about my struggles. Even though the dance world is not your realm, you have embraced my love for it and given me invaluable feedback from your own perspective. Your words are scattered throughout every chapter and raise the level of writing on these pages. You are truly my partner in life, and I could not accomplish anything like this without you.

Finally, thank you to my Father in Heaven for the constant guidance and inspiration. Looking back at every stage, I can see your hand guiding my journey through writing this book. You put the right people in my path at just the right times and gave me the inspiration in the first place.

References

1. (pg. 9) Covey, Stephen R. *The Seven Habits of Highly Effective People: Restoring the Character Ethic*. Simon & Schuster, 1992.

2. (pg, 35) Franklin, Eric N. *Dance Imagery for Technique and Performance*. Second ed., Human Kinetics, pp. 118-119, 2014.

3. (pg. 55) Warren, Gretchen Ward. *Classical Ballet Technique*. University of South Florida Press, pp. 11, 1989.

4. (pg. 67) Lishka, Gerald R. *A handbook for the ballet accompanist*. Indiana University Press, pp. 17, 1979.

5. (pg. 72) Huang, Chungliang Al, and Al Chung-liang Huang. *Thinking Body, Dancing Mind: TaoSports for Extraordinary Performance in Athletics, Business, and Life*. Bantam Books, pp. 46, 1994.

6. (pg. 81) Kondo, Marie. *The Life-Changing Magic of Tidying Up: The Japanese Art of Decluttering and Organizing*. Bolinda Publishing Pty, Limited, 2016.

7. (pg. 85) Warren, Gretchen Ward. *Classical Ballet Technique*. University of South Florida Press, pp. 80, 1989.

8. (pg. 88) Blom, Lynne Anne, and L. Tarin Chaplin. *The Intimate Act Of Choreography*. University of Pittsburgh Press, pp. 13, 1982.

9. *(pg. 114) Progressing Ballet Technique | Excel in Dance Training*, https://www.pbt.dance/en.

10. (pg. 121) Seuss, Dr. *The Foot Book: Dr. Seuss's Wacky Book of Opposites*. Random House, 1996.

11. (pg. 121) Boynton, Sandra. *Belly Button Book! (Oversized Lap Edition)*. Workman Publishing Company, 2011.

12. (pg. 121) Boynton, Sandra. *Barnyard Dance! (Oversized Lap Edition)*. Workman Publishing Company, 2011.

13. (pg. 121) Seuss, Dr. *Oh, the Places You'll Go!* Collins, 1990.

14. (pg. 145) Grant, Gail. *Technical Manual and Dictionary of Classical Ballet*. Third revised ed., Dover Publications, 1982.

15. (pg. 155) Roosevelt, Theodore. *Citizenship in a Republic*. Paris, France, 23 April 1910.

16. (pg. 156) Franklin, Eric N. *Dance Imagery for Technique and Performance*. Second ed., Human Kinetics, 2014.

17. *(pg. 156) Simply On Purpose - Positive Parenting Techniques*, https://simplyonpurpose.org/.

Index

About the Author

Candace Egbert is an experienced dance instructor setting out to smooth the transition from dancer to dance teacher.

Candace graduated with honors from Utah Valley University with a BFA in Dance – Ballet Emphasis. While there, she danced with UVU's resident student ballet company and wrote her honors thesis on improving collegiate dance training. Candace has taught, choreographed and adjudicated dance at local studios, after-school programs, and high schools for the performing arts for over a decade. She is certified in Progressing Ballet Technique, is a member of NDEO, and was also a finalist in Utah Metropolitan Ballet's Choreography Design Project. She also dances and performs with Deseret Dance Theater.

Candace and her husband Chandler have four children and live in Utah.

Visit Amazon.com to read and leave reviews for

Be the Dance Teacher They Remember.

You can also follow Candace on Instagram @candaceegbert and read more insights about this book at

#BetheDanceTeacherTheyRemember.

#BETHEDANCETEACHERTHEYREMEM...

Made in United States
Troutdale, OR
08/26/2023

12387314R00116